Evelyn Findlater's
VEGETARIAN FOOD PROCESSOR

A wealth of recipes and advice to help you make the most of your processor in preparing quick and healthful meals for all occasions and for all the family.

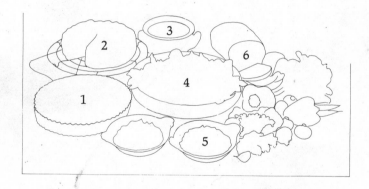

Evelyn Findlater's

VEGETARIAN FOOD PROCESSOR

Quick and Easy Recipes to Make the Most of Your Machine

by

Evelyn Findlater

Illustrated by Peter Kesteven

THORSONS PUBLISHERS LIMITED
Wellingborough, Northamptonshire

Published in co-operation with The Vegetarian Society of the
United Kingdom Ltd., Parkdale, Dunham Road, Altrincham, Cheshire

First published September 1985
Second Impression November 1985

British Library Cataloguing in Publication Data

Findlater, Evelyn
   Evelyn Findlater's vegetarian food processor.
   1. Vegetarian cookery
   2. Food processor cookery
   I. Title   II. Vegetarian Society (UK)
   641.5′636   TX837

   ISBN 0-7225-1113-2

Printed and bound in Great Britain

CONTENTS

INTRODUCTION

Although the recipes in this book were specially created with a food processor in mind they have also been devised with your health and the health and well-being of those you feed as a priority. The book is not just designed for vegetarians, although the recipes are meatless, but to encourage the use of a wider variety of foods in the diet which are high in fibre, low in fats, sugar and salt and with adequate amounts of protein, vitamins and minerals.

There seems to be a mini-explosion taking place today which is exposing how we misuse the abundant supply of foods available, how we eat too many processed, de-vitalized foods which are overloaded with sugar, salt and unmentionable additives, but the adverts still tell us that a large sweetie bar a day 'helps you work, rest and play'. My youngest child was watching her favourite programme the other morning when on came an advert for monster-shaped crisps . Up she jumped, suffused with excitement, cheeks all aglow and rushed upstairs to my eldest son's room. She appeared two minutes later with a handful of these crispy monsters. Of course I let her eat them but, fortunately for her, they are not normal fare. She would have been just as happy with wholewheat monsters flavoured with naturally fermented soya sauce. Thankfully, the food manufacturers are at last getting a thrashing — and not just from health-orientated magazines, but from our national newspapers who now occasionally join in the battle for a healthier diet for all. But we are still being fooled. Our food producers are very quick to catch on to the health food boom. They stick labels on packets and tins saying 'extra fibre' or 'plus extra vitamins' and still cheat us of the earth's bountiful goodness.

Despite all this interference in our foods we are living longer than ever before. But it is not a question of how long we live. Rather more important is what state of health are we enjoying as we trundle along towards a ripe old age? To be happy I think one needs to be healthy. Medical evidence has shown that the body's health, the level of physical and mental energy and even our personal reactions have a direct connection with our diet.

What, then, should we be eating? Well, we all need basically the same nutritional requirements, whether we eat meat or not. It's a question of balance with the right amount of protein and unprocessed carbohydrates and an adequate supply of vitamins and minerals. Research has revealed that today's Western diet is too low in fibre, and is overloaded with saturated fats, sugar and salt, not to mention the additives, and concludes that these factors have become an increasing threat to our health.

I will explain briefly about protein to still your fears in case you should be under the misapprehension that there is any lack of it in a vegetarian diet. Also, I will touch on the subject of fibre, fats, sugar and salt, which are important to know about if you wish to try an alternative way of eating which I feel is not only healthier but encourages a more responsible attitude towards the world we live in. The less meat and more grains, pulses and fresh vegetables we eat, the more chance we have of providing food for all. Take, for example, the simple soya bean. When grown on one acre of land it will yield enough protein for one person for six years. Compare this with animal farming. That very same harvest of beans, fed to animals, will only produce enough protein for one human being for eighty days. I'll let you ponder on that.

Protein

The body does not store protein as it does fats but needs a constant supply, as protein is the builder of all body tissues including muscles, blood, skin, hair, nails, and internal organs such as your heart, brain, liver and kidneys. It also forms hormones, enzymes and antibodies and can, in emergencies, be a source of heat and energy if the body is not taking in enough carbohydrates and fats. However, it is important to balance your protein intake with these warming, energy-giving foods. If the body does not get enough protein it will not sustain proper growth, but if not complemented by energy foods then the protein in muscle tissue can be converted into carbohydrates which, in turn, can lead to protein deficiency.

Not only does the body need protein, but it must be what is termed a 'complete' protein with all the amino acids in balance. There are twenty-two amino acids making up human protein. The body produces fourteen, while the other eight, which are known as essential amino acids, must be obtained from your diet. Meat, fish, dairy produce and the soya bean have these essential amino acids in the necessary proportions, whereas grains, legumes (dried peas, beans and lentils), nuts and seeds are deficient in some of the essential amino acids. For this reason they have been labelled as second-class protein in the past but now, through research, findings have shown that if these foods are complemented in various ways then a proper amino acid balance will be achieved. To obtain enough usable protein you must combine the foods in one of the following ways:

1. Grains with legumes (dried peas, beans or lentils).
2. Grains with nuts or seeds.
3. Grains with dairy produce.
4. Legumes with nuts or seeds.

You can, of course, mix these combinations. For example, a risotto could have grains, beans and a little cheese to top. Proportion-wise, you can't go wrong if the main meal consists of at least fifty per cent grains (remember most grains treble in size when cooked) twenty-five per cent legumes, nuts and seeds or dairy produce, or a combination of all three and the other twenty-five per cent land or sea vegetables either lightly steamed or in a salad.

I have devised the recipes in the book so that you do get a complete protein intake in all lunch and supper dishes. With practice, and a conscious awareness of the food you eat, you will be able to create many variations which will provide all the protein your body needs.

Fibre

Although fibre, which is the structural part of plants, has no nutritional value, it plays a vital part in the elimination of waste matter from the body. With its capacity to absorb water and become sponge-like it helps keep faeces or stools moist and bulky and grips on to the muscles of the colon wall. These muscles can then work efficiently to expel the faeces quickly from the body. If the faeces are hard and small, which happens when one is constipated, then the muscles strain in an effort to contract. This condition, if prolonged, will lead over the years to ruptures in the wall of the gut. The lining of the colon swells through these holes and forms little pouches. These diverticulae or pouches often become inflamed and cause great pain. This disease, which is called diverticulitis, can lead to abscesses and makes elimination impossible and surgery inevitable. Evidence also points to a connection between a low-fibre diet and cancer of the colon. Much research in this field of nutrition has revealed that in countries where the diet is high in fibre this disease is virtually unknown. However, in Western countries, where low-fibre diets are widespread, the incidence of diverticulitis is present in approximately ten per cent of all men and women over the age of forty.

For many years, doctors recommended a low-fibre diet to sufferers of chronic constipation or diverticulitis because it was wrongly thought that fibre would only serve to irritate the inflamed area. Thankfully, now hospitals and doctors are advising high-fibre diets for sufferers of this painful disease, the result of which is that surgery usually becomes unnecessary.

Not only does fibre act as an efficient eliminator, but much evidence has shown that it can alter bacteria in the bowel, making it less prone to disease. But with all the much-needed fuss about fibre, the manufacturers of breakfast cereals are having an economic boom. Packets of bran, wheat fibre and cereals fortified with extra bran line the shelves not only of health food shops but our supermarkets. By itself, bran is pretty unpalatable and in my opinion can ruin a lovely breakfast of muesli and fruit, but the advice is to spoon it on and get it down you, no matter how much you choke. By far the simplest way to eat fibre is to adopt a wholefood diet and eat the stuff as nature intended — unprocessed, unrefined and much more acceptable to the taste buds. Dietary fibre is present only in whole grains, vegetables and fruit. Bran, which is usually the fibre of whole wheat, has been found to be most effective where the bowel movement is concerned. Other grains rich in fibre include brown rice and oatmeal. Dried peas, beans and lentils, jacket potatoes, apples, bananas and blackberries are also particularly fibre-rich foods.

Fats

Through much research, by eminent nutritionists, it is now generally accepted that there is a clear connection between a high intake of saturated fats and coronary heart disease. If eaten in large amounts these fats produce too high a level of cholesterol in the blood which, observation has revealed, can make us more vulnerable not only to heart attack, but also to thrombosis, gallstones and illnesses akin to these. In the United Kingdom, disease of the heart is the main cause of death of men between the ages of forty-five and fifty-five.

Saturated fats: include animal fats such as lard, cheese, butter and cream. Palm oil and some vegetable oils containing palm oil are often highly saturated. Also, contrary to general belief, some margarines have a high level of saturated fats unless the label states 'high in polyunsaturates'. No wonder there is a big controversy as to whether we should eat butter or margarine. Just choose those which do have the advisable label and spread lightly, on *wholemeal* bread of course.

Polyunsaturated fats: on the other hand, are high in linoleic acid which helps control the level of cholesterol in the blood. These include safflower seed oil (highest in linoleic acid), sunflower oil, corn oil, wheatgerm oil, soya oil, sesame seed oil and some margarines marked 'high in polyunsaturates'. Olive oil contains what are called mono-unsaturated fatty acids which do not contribute to heart disease. Although it is low in linoleic acid, it has been found to increase the absorption of vitamins A, D, E and K and is completely digestible.

There are three different grades of oil which I think it is important to know about. These are refined, semi-refined and cold-pressed. Refined oils are subjected to high temperatures in order to quicken the process of extraction, which kills valuable nutrients. They often have added chemicals. Semi-refined oils still contain some nutrients as the oil is not so crudely extracted and there are no additives. I use these for deep frying. Finally there are cold-pressed oils which are simply pressed slowly from the seed. They retain their nutrients, have a beautiful aroma and delicious taste and are great for salads and light sautéing. You can also obtain cold-pressed margarine from health stores, which is high in polyunsaturates, has no colouring or additives and has a superb flavour.

My advice, then, is to cut down on saturated fats wherever possible, choose polyunsaturated fats and try those wonderful cold-pressed oils which will not only enhance your food but help keep you fit.

Sugar

Years ago, when I began to read about nutrition and was slowly changing our diet, there came the first time I filled my sugar jar with sticky brown Muscovado sugar. I remember that I felt really wise and good. In those days we were told it was superior to white sugar, but not the truth that all sugar is bad for us no matter what form it takes. But I must admit that if I had known ten years ago, or even three years ago, what I know now I would not have been able to convert my family, and later my students, to wholefood cookery so easily. I made delicious cakes with that brown gooey mass. Nobody noticed that I had substituted wholemeal flour for white, added ground nuts and seeds and more unusual dried fruits, or that carob powder was the chocolate flavour (see notes on carob, page 170). Regardless of the sugar content these cakes were a vast improvement nutritionally on my previous efforts — those wonderful melt-in-the-mouth gateaux and pastries — and were enjoyed without criticism. I can only say from experience that change must be gradual. An imperceptible decrease spread over months will wean the palate and slowly educate it to appreciate less sweet foods.

Why cut down or cut out sugar? For a start, it is the main cause of dental decay. The bacteria in the mouth are nourished by sugar and produce an acid which dissolves tooth enamel. Now the enamel will be restored if given a long enough rest between sweet treats, but today's Western diet does not give this process a chance.

Sugar (sucrose) is considered by experts in the field of nutritional research to be a major cause of obesity, heart disease, diabetes and other digestive disorders. Anything labelled jam has to contain at least sixty per cent sugar by law, many chutneys are fifty to sixty per cent pure sucrose, bought cakes and biscuits not only have a high sugar content but are high in saturated fats and very low in fibre, as lard and white flour is used.

Unfortunately, honey and concentrated fruit sugars are not much better for us, but fructose, as pointed out in the introduction to the Desserts and Puddings chapter, looks like caster sugar, is absorbed more slowly from the intestinal tract than sucrose (ordinary sugar) and therefore does not cause the blood sugar to rise as sharply. It is also a third sweeter than sucrose and so you use less.

So it would seem sensible to use sugar and all sweeteners as an occasional treat rather than a regular part of your diet.

Salt (Sodium Chloride)

We do not need salt in the isolated state we are used to, plonked in the centre of the table and used far too liberally on our home-cooked food, as well as in bought bread, cheese, ham, canned meats and vegetables and, sadly, in baby foods. Findings have shown that excessive salt intake — which we in the West indulge in by around twenty times our body's tolerance — overloads the system with sodium and upsets the balance with potassium; it robs calcium from bones and teeth and can cause damage to the heart, kidneys, bladder, arteries, veins and the nervous system. Sea salt has only a slightly lower sodium content than ordinary salt and should still be only very sparingly used.

I have included both sugar and salt in my recipes because many of you will be new to wholefoods, which I feel is enough to be getting on with. Use more herbs and spices in your food and less salt and you will begin to taste the flavour of the food without the need to rely on the salt.

Why use a food processor?
My food processor has become invaluable to me over the last few months. I'm not a machine person — at least I wasn't until the discipline of my work and lack of time forced me to seek the help of a few kitchen aids. In fact, since I first became enthusiastic about cooking at the age of sixteen I have worked mainly with my hands, and they show it! Before my processor, my gadgets consisted of a few chopping knives, a garlic crusher, a hand-operated egg whisk and a liquidizer. Now I wonder how I ever managed. My hands feel less like sandpaper, my wrists have stopped aching, I save time and I work more creatively.

I'm sure there are many people who have a fear of machines or are under the misapprehension that they're more bother than they're worth. Well I've changed my mind — although I still enjoy touching the food I'm preparing, and fulfil that need from time to time by making a batch of bread by hand, I wouldn't be without my processor. Not only is it an efficient time-saver, it is also an aid to better nutrition. It chops vegetables very finely in seconds, thus cutting down cooking time with the result that soups and purées retain their full flavour and valuable nutrients which are often destroyed by over-cooking. Sauces and batters are made simply by putting all the ingredients into the processor bowl and blending together in seconds to a perfect consistency. The sauce then needs only two minutes to cook. Bread takes sixty seconds to knead, if your machine has that facility, instead of seven to ten minutes and the most delicious whips and other light desserts can be created by the press of a button.

What better aid, when life is hectic? But remember, you are the master of your machine, so use it to help take the chore out of an everyday duty which can sometimes be a pain although at others times a real joy, whether you use a machine, the touch of a hand or, even better, both.

You will no doubt receive a booklet with your processor which will give you explicit directions on assembling and servicing it and how to connect it to power. However, I think it is worth passing on some tips which have proved useful to me in making the most of my machine.

Steel blades
This attachment is the most important and versatile of all. The texture you get is determined by the length of time you allow for processing. For a coarse texture use the *pulse* facility which allows the cutting blades to operate in a start-stop

action. This helps you to control the texture of certain foods. Use these blades for the following foods.

Vegetables: Cut hard vegetables such as potatoes, carrots and celery into small chunks. Put into the processor bowl and process for approximately 10 seconds. For softer vegetables like peppers, mushrooms and skinned tomatoes process for a few seconds only. Any longer for peppers and mushrooms and you will have a paste. When making soups or Bolognese sauce, process the vegetables before cooking; this saves time and nourishment.

Bread and yeasted doughs: Put flour and dry ingredients into the bowl and process for a few seconds. Then quickly pour the liquid down the feed tube while the motor is on and continue to process until a dough is formed. If you wish to make a large batch for freezing, check first the maximum quantity your machine will take. I find it much easier to mix all ingredients by hand to form a dough, break the dough into equal pieces of less than the maximum quantity and then knead each in the processor. Let the machine rest for 30 minutes after using to make larger amounts of dough.

Crumbs, either biscuit or bread: Break up into smallish pieces and process until fine.

Pastry: Blend margarine, water and a little of the flour until creamy. Gradually add wholemeal flour through feed tube while motor is still on. Chill in a polythene bag for 30 minutes before rolling out.

Nuts and seeds: Process. If a recipe calls for a mixture of nuts and seeds the texture of medium to fine breadcrumbs, then do the seeds separately as these take less time to process.

Cakes: The processor will not 'cream' magarine and sugar to the light and fluffy consistency necessary in making light sponges. It does, however, 'cream' well enough to achieve a texture similar to Madeira cake. A satisfactory sponge-type cake can be made using the 'all in one' method — place all the ingredients in the bowl and process until smooth.

When making fruit cakes the dried fruit is added after other ingredients are blended. Use *pulse* only when adding fruit. Using the speed buttons will chop the fruit too finely.

Sauces: For a plain white sauce simply put all ingredients into the bowl and process until smooth. Transfer the mixture to a saucepan, bring to the boil and cook for 2 minutes, stirring constantly.

For onion, parsley or mushroom sauce, chop roughly and process with other ingredients.

For cheese sauce stir the grated cheese into the hot sauce when cooked.

For apple sauce, core *unpeeled* cooking apples and chop roughly. Cook with apple juice concentrate and a little water until soft. Process the hot apples until smooth.

Batters: Place dry ingredients, egg if called for in the recipe, and half the liquid into the bowl. Process until well blended then gradually pour in the remaining liquid through the feed tube with the motor on. (Best results are achieved if the batter is allowed to stand for at least 20 minutes before using.)

Slicing plate

You can determine the thickness of slices of vegetables and fruit by the amount of pressure exerted on the pusher. For thickish slices press firmly down, but for general purposes push with moderate force.

To slice round vegetables and fruit, such as potatoes, onions, peppers and apples, after peeling, de-seeding and coring etc., cut in half lengthwise and fit each half into the feed tube in an upright position and push with an even pressure. Cut larger vegetables and fruit to fit snugly into the feed tube.

Slice mushrooms by placing them with their caps to the outside of the feed tube, insert food pusher and process, pushing with an even pressure.

For slicing long vegetables and fruit, such as carrots, cucumber, celery and bananas, cut to a length slightly shorter than the feed tube. Stand upright, packing solidly to fill tube, and process while pressing either firmly or moderately, depending on the thickness you require.

To slice red or white cabbage for coleslaw, cut cabbage vertically into wedges, then cut into smaller sections to fit feed tube. Stand cabbage upright and slice, using moderate pressure.

Shredding plate

This will grate carrots, potatoes, apples, cheese and other similar textured foods. Cut pieces off to fit the feed tube and press firmly down with the pusher.

For grating cheese, cut into pieces to fit the feed tube, and process using the pusher.

Egg white whisk

Use for egg whites only. Do not use with liquids. Whisk up to six egg whites. To achieve a stiff, peaking consistency, process for approximately 3 minutes. Not all processors have this attachment.

It is important not to overload the processor.

Until you are used to your processor, process food briefly and check the consistency as it is very easy to over-process foods. And, most important, keep your processor on the worktop ready to use, otherwise it will most probably end up in the corner of a cupboard, which seems a pity as it really is a most useful and efficient kitchen aid.

I.

SOUPS, DIPS, PURÉES AND PÂTÉS

I think I had most enjoyment with my food processor in devising the recipes in this chapter. No more sieving vegetables to make smooth soups and pâtés. Dishes I had prepared in the past took on a richer, more full-bodied flavour and were, because of the shorter cooking time required, nutritionally more valuable.

With a little imagination and the right combination of fresh vegetables, pulses and other wholesome ingredients, the variations of which are endless, you can achieve the most wonderful flavours. My choice will, I hope, not only delight your palate but add those vital nutrients to your diet which go a long way towards creating a fit and healthy body.

Soups

One sees in many cookbooks the use of stock in soup. Well, stock which is either obtained from a mixture of odd left-over vegetables or vegetable cooking water is, I think, invaluable for making gravy or a mixed vegetable soup, but can affect the subtlety of other more delicate flavours. The choice of vegetables and herbs should complement each other to give an individual distinctive flavour of their own. For instance, cabbage water, carrot and onion water which could be the basis of a particular stock would completely spoil a delicate flavoured soup like Chick Pea and Mint, but would blend extremely well into the Pot Barley Broth. Stock is invaluable but should be used with discretion. I use herb salt or vegetable stock cubes, both of which are quite mild and enhance the flavour of the vegetables rather than overpower them.

Hot Soups

Lentil and Miso Soup

This wholesome and very nutritious soup is one of my favourites. It is a meal in itself. The combination of lentils with the miso, a soya bean paste rich in protein, makes a complete protein food. Miso has a salty flavour so no salt is needed in the recipe. It must be added at the end of cooking time or you destroy its valuable nutrients.

Imperial (Metric)	American
2 medium onions, peeled	2 medium onions, peeled
2 cloves garlic, peeled	2 cloves garlic, peeled
3 sticks celery, washed	3 stalks celery, washed
2 large carrots, scraped	2 large carrots, scraped
5 oz (140g) red split lentils	¾ cup red split lentils
2 pints (1.1 litres) boiling water	5 cups boiling water
2 tablespoons tomato purée	2 tablespoons tomato paste
Few sprigs fresh parsley	Few sprigs fresh parsley
2 slightly rounded tablespoons miso	2 slightly rounded tablespoons miso
Freshly ground black pepper	Freshly ground black pepper

1 Cut onion roughly into 8 pieces. Slice garlic. Chop celery into approx. 1½ inch (3.5cm) lengths, leaving as much green on as possible.

2 With *steel blades* in position put onion, garlic and celery into the processor bowl. Chop. Scoop out and place in a medium-sized heavy bottomed saucepan.

3 Slice carrots lengthwise then into approximately 1 inch (2.5cm) long sticks. Put in the processor bowl with steel blades still in position. Chop. Put this in the saucepan. (No need to wash processor bowl as you will need it to liquidize the soup later.)

4 Wash lentils, picking over for small stones (a sieve is best. Just let cold water flow over the lentils for half a minute.). Drain the lentils and add to the vegetables.

5 Add the boiling water, tomato purée and parsley. Stir well and bring to boil. Simmer for 20 minutes only.

6 Put miso in a small bowl. Stir in some of the hot soup liquid and cream the mixture together. Pour into the soup, stirring well. With *steel blades* in position, purée the soup, four ladles at a time, until smooth.

7 Pour back into the saucepan, add freshly ground black pepper and heat through but do not boil.

Chick Pea and Mint Soup

A refreshing and tasty Middle Eastern-style soup which is best served with Wholemeal Pitta Bread, see page 161 for recipe, or Granary French Loaf, see page 157 for recipe.

Imperial (Metric)	American
8 oz (225g) dry weight chick peas	1½ cups dry garbanzo beans
I teaspoon sea salt	I teaspoon sea salt
2 tablespoons fresh mint	2 tablespoons fresh mint
2 large cloves garlic, peeled	2 large cloves garlic, peeled
3 tablespoons olive oil	3 tablespoons olive oil
I teaspoon coriander seeds, crushed	I teaspoon coriander seeds, crushed
Juice of I lemon	Juice of I lemon
Freshly ground black pepper	Freshly ground black pepper

1 Wash chick peas (garbanzo beans) and pick over for stones. Soak in 2 pints (5 cups) cold water for 8 hours, changing the water three times.

2 Cook the peas (beans) in plenty of fresh water for 1 to 1½ hours until soft. Add the sea salt 10 minutes before end of cooking time.

3 Drain, reserving the cooking water. Add enough hot water to bring the level up to 1¾ pints (1 litre/4 cups).

4 Put peas (beans), water, mint, garlic and 2 tablespoons olive oil into a bowl. With *steel blades* in position, purée the pea (bean) mixture, 3 ladles at a time, until quite smooth.

5 Put the remaining tablespoon of oil into a clean, dry saucepan and lightly toast the crushed coriander seeds, but do not burn.

6 Now pour the chick pea (garbanzo) mixture into the saucepan. Stir in the lemon juice and freshly ground black pepper to taste. Bring to boil and let simmer with the lid on for 10 minutes only.

Note: To serve, dot with a few young tops of mint which look like small green roses, or just with a little chopped mint.

Beetroot (Beet) and Fennel Soup

This is my version of Russian Borsch. It is traditionally served with sour cream, but I make my own cream by adding two tablespoons double (heavy) cream to ¼ pint (140ml/⅔ cup) thick natural yogurt. Whisk the cream to a firm consistency, stir into the yogurt and leave to chill in the refrigerator for one hour.

Imperial (Metric)	American
I onion (6oz/170g weight after peeling and roughly chopping)	I onion (6 ounces weight after peeling and roughly chopping)
4 oz (115g) fennel root, roughly chopped	I cup roughly chopped fennel root
3 cardamom seeds, podded	3 cardamom seeds, podded
2 tablespoons vegetable oil	2 tablespoons vegetable oil
2 medium potatoes, scrubbed (approx. 8 oz/225g in weight)	2 medium potatoes, scrubbed (approx. 8 ounces in weight)
I lb (455g) raw beetroot (weight after thinly peeling and chopping)	2¾ cups thinly peeled and chopped raw beets
1¾ pints (I litre) boiling water	4 cups boiling water
1½ teaspoons herb salt *or*	1½ teaspoons herb salt *or*
1½ vegetable stock cubes	1½ vegetable stock cubes
I bay leaf	I bay leaf
I tablespoon cider vinegar	I tablespoon cider vinegar
½ teaspoon freshly ground black pepper	½ teaspoon freshly ground black pepper
5 oz (140g) carton thick natural yogurt plus 2 tablespoons double cream, mixed together	I cup thick plain yogurt plus 2 tablespoons heavy cream, mixed together
A little freshly chopped parsley to garnish	A little fresh chopped parsley to garnish

1 Set *steel blades* in place. Put the roughly chopped onion, chopped fennel and the crushed cardamom seeds in the processor bowl. Chop.

2 Heat oil in a heavy bottomed saucepan. Sauté the onion, fennel and cardamoms for 6 minutes with lid on.

3 Cut scrubbed potatoes into approx. 1 inch (2.5cm) pieces. Set *steel blades* in place and chop beetroot (beets) and potatoes.

4 Add boiling water and herb salt or stock cubes to the sautéd onion and fennel mixture. Next add the beetroot (beets), potato, bay leaf, cider vinegar and freshly ground black pepper.

5 Bring to boil and then turn down to simmer. Put the lid on and simmer for 25 minutes only.

6 With *steel blades* in place blend the soup to a purée, adding 4 ladles of the mixture at a time to the processor bowl.

7 Re-heat but do not boil. Pour into the serving bowl. Drop the yogurt and cream mixture into the centre. Sprinkle with a little chopped parsley. Stir in just before serving.

Sprouted Soya Bean, Lemon and Parsley Soup

This soup is jam-packed with goodness. The soya bean is a complete protein and sprouted it is very digestible and has a pleasant, sweet, nutty flavour. See notes on the soya bean and making soya cheese (Tofu) on page 38, also Sprouted Bean Spread on page 30. You have to prepare this soup a few days in advance because the beans take 3 to 4 days to sprout.

Imperial (Metric)	American
6 oz (170g) dry weight soya beans	I cupful dry soy beans
I bunch spring onions	I bunch scallions
4 oz (115g) very small, button mushrooms	2 cups very small button mushrooms
2 level teaspoons herb salt	2 level teaspoons herb salt
6 tablespoons fresh chopped parsley	6 tablespoons fresh chopped parsley
Juice of 2 lemons	Juice of 2 lemons
Freshly ground black pepper to taste	Freshly ground black pepper to taste

1 To sprout the beans, wash well and pick over for stones. Cover with 1½ pints (850ml/3¾ cups) cold water and let them soak for 12 hours. Change the water three times. Drain the beans and place in a large jar. Cover the top with a piece of muslin secured with an elastic band. Put in a warm place (an airing cupboard is perfect). Pour 1 pint (570ml/2½ cups) of cold water on them three times a day. Drain the water through the muslin. Do this until the beans have ½ inch (1.5cm) sprouts. Takes about 3 to 4 days.

2 Cook sprouted beans for 2 hours or more until soft. (Or pressure cook for 30 minutes.)

3 Measure out 2 pints (5 cups) boiling water, including any cooking water. Put *steel blades* in position. To one cup of sprouted beans add one cup boiling water and purée until smooth. Continue to do this until you have puréed all the beans.

4 Now put the remaining hot water into a heavy-bottomed saucepan. Bring to boil and pour the bean mixture into this.

5 Chop the spring onions (scallions) using all the green. Slice the mushrooms in three. Add these, with herb salt, parsley and lemon juice, to the soup. Stir well. Now add the freshly ground black pepper.

6 Continue to simmer for 10 more minutes. Serve with oven toasted wholemeal bread, which is simply finger slices of bread spread with polyunsaturated margarine and baked in the oven until crisp at 375°F/190°C (Gas Mark 5) for 20 minutes. You can rub with garlic before baking and sprinkle with naturally fermented soya sauce for really tasty toasted fingers.

Pot Barley Broth

This is a warming, tasty and very satisfying soup. Just right for those cold winter days. Use pot barley which is the whole grain. Pearl barley is processed so it is without the bran (fibre) and has very little germ left. Do not add salt as shoyu and miso are salty enough.

Imperial (Metric)	American
3 oz (85g) pot barley	⅓ cup pot barley
I large onion	I large onion
2 cloves garlic	2 cloves garlic
3 tablespoons sunflower oil	3 tablespoons sunflower oil
3 medium carrots, scraped	3 medium carrots, scraped
2 medium potatoes, scrubbed	2 medium potatoes, scrubbed
3 sticks celery	3 stalks celery
I lb (455g) ripe soft tomatoes (tinned will do)	I pound ripe soft tomatoes (canned will do)
I heaped teaspoon *sweet* mixed herbs	I heaped teaspoon *sweet* mixed herbs
I bay leaf	I bay leaf
Handful parsley, chopped	Handful parsley, chopped
I level tablespoon miso (soya bean paste)	I level tablespoon miso (soya bean paste)
I tablespoon shoyu (naturally fermented soya sauce)	I tablespoon naturally fermented soy sauce
Freshly ground black pepper to taste	Freshly ground black pepper to taste

1 Wash the barley and soak in 1 pint (570ml/2½ cups) cold water for at least 4 hours, or overnight.

2 Drain the liquid into a measuring jug and add enough water to a level of 1½ pints (850ml/3¾ cups).

3 Set *shredding plate* in position. Cut onion and garlic lengthwise in quarters. Pack into the feed tube and push down with an even pressure to slice. Scoop out.

4 Heat oil in a heavy-bottomed saucepan. Sauté onion and garlic for 7 minutes until soft. Stir in the drained barley and continue to cook for 3 more minutes.

5 Now add the reserved water. Bring to boil and simmer for 20 minutes with lid on.

6 In the meantime, cut carrots in half width-wise and then in half lengthwise. Set the *slicing plate* in position. Pack into feed tube and slice. Cut potatoes in half or quarters. Pack into the feed tube and slice. Cut celery in lengths just shorter than that of the feed tube. Pack well in and slice.

7 Scoop out the chopped vegetables and add them with the herbs, bay leaf and parsley to the cooking barley. Continue to simmer for a further 10 minutes.

8 Skin the tomatoes, if fresh, by first cutting a thin circle around the stalk bases, immerse in boiling water for 5 minutes. Peel off skins.

9 Set *steel blades* in position and purée the tomatoes until smooth. Add this to the soup. Bring to boil and let simmer for 10 more minutes only.

10 Finally, put miso and shoyu (soy sauce) into a small bowl, blend with a little of the soup liquid to a smooth consistency. Pour this into the cooked soup. Add the freshly ground black pepper. Taste and add more shoyu if not salty enough.

Note: Serve with toasted wholemeal bread and a choice of cheeses for a hearty lunch or on its own as a real winter warmer.

Chilled Soups

Vichyssoise (Cream of Leek and Potato Soup)

This very popular soup is traditionally served chilled, but I like it hot or cold.

Note: To get 1 pound (455g) leeks after trimming you usually have to buy 2 pounds (900g), depending on the weight of the coarse green ends.

Imperial (Metric)	American
1 lb (455g) leeks (weight when trimmed and washed)	1 pound leeks (weight when trimmed and washed)
1 lb (455g) potatoes, scrubbed	1 pound potatoes, scrubbed
2 tender sticks celery	2 tender stalks celery
3 tablespoons sunflower oil	3 tablespoons sunflower oil
¾ pint (425ml) water	2 cups water
¾ pint (425)ml) milk	2 cups milk
2 tablespoons freshly chopped parsley	2 tablespoons freshly chopped parsley
1 rounded teaspoon herb salt *or* sea salt	1 rounded teaspoon herb salt *or* sea salt
Freshly ground black pepper to taste	Freshly ground black pepper to taste
½ teaspoon freshly grated nutmeg	½ teaspoon freshly grated nutmeg
8 fl oz (230ml) single cream	1 cupful light cream
Garnish of a few chopped green leaves from the celery tops	Garnish of a few chopped green leaves from the celery tops

1 Trim the leeks by topping and tailing. Do this by cutting a shallow indent around the area where the coarser end of the leaves begin. Inside these you will find tender green parts. Leave this attached to the white head. Wash well. Cut into lengths just shorter than that of the feed tube.

2 Cut scrubbed potatoes in halves or quarters, depending on size. Cut celery sticks into lengths just shorter than the feed tube.

3 Set *slicing plate* in position. Slice the prepared vegetables, packing well into the feed tube and pushing with an even pressure.

4 Heat oil in a heavy-bottomed saucepan. Sauté the sliced vegetables for 5 minutes.

5 Add the water, milk, parsley, salt, black pepper and nutmeg. Bring to boil. Turn down to simmer and leave for 20 minutes only.

6 Set *steel blades* in position and blend the cooked soup, four ladles at a time, until quite smooth.

7 Stir in the cream. Taste and adjust seasoning. If you wish to eat this hot, re-heat but do not boil again. If it is to be eaten chilled then refrigerate for at least 2 hours. Sprinkle on the chopped celery leaves just before serving.

Note: The cream is a luxury addition, but the soup will still be delicious if you add 3 rounded tablespoons dried skimmed milk powder. Blend this with the milk in the recipe to give a creamy effect. You might have to add a little more water if soup is too thick.

Spanish Salad Soup

Exciting and different, this is a must for days when lunch is eaten in the garden. The Spanish Soup is served chilled with a choice of garnishes, including chopped vegetables, olives and croûtons.

Imperial (Metric)	American
4 thick slices wholemeal bread	4 thick slices wholewheat bread
I large Spanish onion, peeled	I large Spanish onion, peeled
I small red pepper, de-seeded	I small red pepper, de-seeded
I small green pepper, de-seeded	I small green pepper, de-seeded
2 medium courgettes	2 medium zucchini
3 tablespoons olive oil	3 tablespoons olive oil
2 cloves garlic, peeled and crushed	2 cloves garlic, peeled and crushed
I lb (455g) ripe, soft tomatoes	I pound ripe, soft tomatoes
2 tablespoons tomato purée	2 tablespoons tomato paste
3 tablespoons mayonnaise	3 tablespoons mayonnaise
Approx. ¾ pint (425ml) iced water	Approx. 2 cupfuls iced water
Sea salt and freshly ground black pepper to taste	Sea salt and freshly ground black pepper to taste

1 Set *steel blades* in position. Break bread up roughly. Put into the mixing bowl and process until the bread is in small crumbs. Scoop out and put in a large mixing bowl.

2 Set *slicing plate* in position. Cut onion lengthwise in quarters, pack lengthwise into feed tube and push with an even pressure to slice. Continue with the peppers, cutting them in half lengthwise, then the courgettes (zucchini), cutting these first in half width-wise then in half lengthwise.

3 Heat oil in a heavy-bottomed saucepan. Sauté the onion, garlic, peppers and courgettes (zucchini) for 7 minutes with lid on. Scoop out and put in the mixing bowl with the breadcrumbs.

4 Meanwhile, skin the tomatoes by cutting a circle around the edge of the stalk area. Immerse in boiling water for 5 minutes. Peel off skins.

5 Set *steel blades* in position and purée the tomatoes with the tomato purée (paste) and ½ pint (285ml/1⅓ cups) water until smooth. Pour this over the breadcrumb mixture. Mix well together.

6 Still using *steel blades,* pour half this mixture into the processor bowl and blend until smooth. Then blend the other half of the mixture.

7 Place in a serving bowl. Stir in the mayonnaise and enough iced water to give the consistency of a thin batter or single (light) cream. Season with sea salt and freshly ground black pepper. Chill well before serving.

Garnishes for Spanish Salad Soup:
These are arranged in separate bowls and spooned into individual portions of the soup when ready to eat.

I suggest small bowls of onion rings, chopped cucumber, lightly cooked French beans (cut ½ inch/1.5cm long), stoned olives and croûtons.

Carrot Cooler

Absolutely delicious and very simple to prepare. Best with young, home-grown, new-season carrots.

Imperial (Metric)	American
I medium onion, skinned	I medium onion, skinned
2 tablespoons safflower oil	2 tablespoons safflower oil
I large clove garlic, crushed	I large clove garlic, crushed
I½ lbs (680g) young carrots, scrubbed	I½ pounds young carrots, scrubbed
½ teaspoon dried tarragon	½ teaspoon dried tarragon
I½ pints (850ml) water	3¾ cups water
I½ vegetable stock cubes	I½ vegetable stock cubes
¼ pint (140ml) double cream	⅓ cup heavy cream
Freshly ground black pepper	Freshly ground black pepper
2 oz (55g) shelled pistachio nuts	½ cup shelled pistachio nuts
I tablespoon fresh chopped parsley	I tablespoon fresh chopped parsley

1 Set *slicing plate* in position. Cut onion in half and pack into the feed tube. Slice. Scoop out and leave plate in position.

2 Heat oil in a heavy-bottomed saucepan. Sauté the sliced onion and crushed garlic on low heat for 7 minutes with lid on.

3 Meanwhile slice the carrots, packing them well into the feed tube lengthwise.

4 Sauté these with the onion for another 7 minutes with lid on. Stir in the tarragon at this stage.

5 Bring water to boil. Stir in the stock cubes and pour this into the cooking vegetables. Let simmer on low heat for 20 minutes.

6 Set *steel blades* in position. Purée the soup, 4 ladles at a time, until quite smooth.

7 Whisk the cream until it holds its shape but is still soft.

8 Stir this into the soup. Taste and add freshly ground black pepper and a little sea salt if needed. Place in a serving bowl and chill for 1 hour in the refrigerator.

To garnish: Finely grind the shelled pistachio nuts. Mix them with very finely chopped, towel-dried parsley and a little freshly ground black pepper. Sprinkle this over the chilled soup just before serving.

Dips, Purées and Pâtés

The exciting variety of dips, purées and pâtés to be made from fresh vegetables, fruit, dried peas and beans, nuts and seeds and dairy produce is endless. Combining these foods with fresh or dried herbs and spices, cold-pressed oils, garlic and lemon juice, you can create some superb tasting dishes from the simple to the exotic.

The recipes that follow can be eaten as appetizing starters with crudités (firm fresh vegetables cut in 2 inch/5 cm matchstick shapes), or spooned onto crisp lettuce leaves or stuffed in wholemeal pitta bread (see page 161 for recipe) for a really healthy lunchtime filler.

Avocado Dip (Gaucamole)

Imperial (Metric)	American
2 large ripe avocado pears	2 large ripe avocado pears
1 small green pepper, de-seeded and roughly chopped	1 small green pepper, de-seeded and roughly chopped
½ small onion, roughly chopped	½ small onion, roughly chopped
1 large clove garlic, crushed	1 large clove garlic, crushed
1 tablespoon lemon juice	1 tablespoon lemon juice
¼ teaspoon sea salt	¼ teaspoon sea salt
¼ teaspoon freshly ground black pepper	¼ teaspoon freshly ground black pepper
Good pinch cayenne pepper	Good pinch cayenne pepper
2 heaped tablespoons yogurt cheese (see page 36)	2 heaped tablespoons yogurt cheese (see page 36)
Few drops Tabasco sauce	Few drops Tabasco sauce

1 With a sharp knife make a small indent in the avocados from the base to the stalk end as if you are going to cut in quarters. The skins will peel off easily if the avocados are ripe. Now cut right through to the centre and each quarter will fall away from the stone quite easily. Chop roughly.

2 Set *steel blades* in position, put all the ingredients except the Tabasco sauce and yogurt cheese into the processor bowl and blend.

3 Scoop out and stir in the yogurt cheese. Taste. Add more seasoning if you wish. Add a few drops of Tabasco sauce and chill for 30 minutes.

Variation:

Avocado and Flageolet Bean Purée: This purée is a variation of the Avocado Dip but has 4 oz (115g) dry weight flageolet beans added. Flageolet beans are young kidney beans. They have a delicate flavour and blend well with avocados.

1 Wash the beans and pick over for stones. Soak overnight, changing the water three times.

2 Bring to boil in fresh water and let simmer for approximately 40 minutes until soft. Add ½ teaspoon sea salt 10 minutes before the end of cooking time. Drain and let cool.

3 With *steel blades* in position, purée until smooth. Stir into the avocado dip just before adding the yogurt cheese and Tabasco. You will need a little more seasoning, so adjust to your own taste.

Simple Aubergine Purée

This is a very simple purée originating from the Middle East. There the aubergines would be split and cooked over charcoal, which gives a smoky taste to the pulp. I bake mine in the oven for a very tasty resulting purée.

Imperial (Metric)	American
3 medium aubergines, approx. 8 oz (225g) each in weight	3 medium eggplants, approx. 8 ounces each in weight
2 cloves garlic, peeled and crushed	2 cloves garlic, peeled and crushed
2 tablespoons lemon juice	2 tablespoons lemon juice
3 tablespoons olive oil	3 tablespoons olive oil
2 level tablespoons ground almonds	2 level tablespoons ground almonds
Sea salt and freshly ground black pepper	Sea salt and freshly ground black pepper

1 Oil the aubergines (eggplants) and bake at 375°F/190°C (Gas Mark 5) for 45 minutes. Leave to cool. Cut the skins and scoop out the pulp.

2 With *steel blades* in position, blend the pulp with the garlic, lemon juice and olive oil until smooth. Scoop out. Stir in the ground almonds.

3 Season with sea salt and freshly ground black pepper. Chill before serving.

Spicy Lentil and Mushroom Pâté

This pâté is rather like a very thick, firm dhal. In fact, adding more liquid to it would make it a perfect dhal to accompany a vegetable curry. You can use whole continental green lentils or the more common red split lentils (split peas).

Imperial (Metric)	American
8 oz (225g) continental green or red split lentils	I cup green or red split lentils
1½ pints (850ml) water	3¾ cups water
I teaspoon sea salt	I teaspoon sea salt
4 oz (115g) small button mushrooms	2 cups small button mushrooms
3 tablespoons peanut or sunflower oil	3 tablespoons peanut or sunflower oil
I clove garlic	I clove garlic
½ teaspoon ground cumin	½ teaspoon ground cumin
I teaspoon coriander seeds, crushed	I teaspon coriander seeds, crushed
½ teaspoon black mustard seeds, crushed	½ teaspoon black mustard seeds, crushed
I level teaspoon turmeric	I level teaspoon turmeric
I dessertspoon grated fresh ginger root	2 teaspoons grated fresh ginger root
I small green chilli, de-seeded and chopped	I small green chili, de-seeded and chopped
2 tablespoons tomato purée	2 tablespoons tomato paste
Juice of 2 limes *or* I large lemon	Juice of 2 limes *or* I large lemon
I small cooking apple, thinly peeled, cored and chopped	I small cooking apple, thinly peeled, cored and chopped

1 Wash the lentils and pick over carefully for grit and small stones.

2 Bring to boil in the water with the salt. Let simmer for 15 minutes if red split lentils, 20 minutes for the continental lentils (or until soft but not too mushy). Drain and let stand in a colander until drained off, saving 2 tablespoons of the cooking liquid.

3 Set *slicing plate* in position. Wash and wipe the mushrooms and slice. Sauté the mushrooms in 2 tablespoons of the oil until soft. Take out and put aside. Add the remaining 1 tablespoon oil to the pan. Fry the garlic, spices, ginger and chilli for 2 minutes (do not allow to burn).

4 With *steel blades* in position, put tomato purée (paste), the fried spices, lime *or* lemon juice and chopped apple into the processor bowl. Blend until smooth. (You might have to add the 2 tablespoons of lentil cooking water if the mixture is not blending easily.) Scoop out into a serving bowl. Stir in the mushrooms. Now mix with the cooked lentils.

Note: This makes a beautiful stuffing for courgettes (zucchini) or marrow (squash). Another idea is to spread thickly on toast, sprinkle with a little grated cheese and put under the grill until lightly browned for a quick lunch or supper dish.

Aubergine Purée with Mushrooms

This is a rich purée, quite delicious and simple to prepare.

Imperial (Metric)	American
3 medium aubergines, approx. 8 oz (225g) each in weight	3 medium eggplants, approx. 8 ounces each in weight
1 medium onion	1 medium onion
¼ lb (115g) small button mushrooms	2 cups small button mushrooms
2 tablespoons olive oil	2 tablespoons olive oil
5 oz (140g) carton sour cream	⅔ cup sour cream
Sea salt and freshly ground black pepper	Sea salt and freshly ground black pepper

1 Oil the aubergines (eggplants). Bake in oven at 375°F/190°C (Gas Mark 5) for 45 minutes. Cut and scoop out the pulp. Let cool.

2 Set *slicing plate* in position. Cut onion in half, pack into the feed tube and slice.

3 Wash mushrooms. Towel dry and slice.

4 Sauté the onion in the oil for 5 minutes. Add the mushrooms and fry for 3 minutes.

5 With *steel blades* in position, blend the aubergine (eggplant) pulp with the onions and mushrooms until smooth. Scoop out and place in a mixing bowl.

6 Stir in the sour cream and season with sea salt and pepper to taste. Chill before serving.

Sprouted Soya Bean Spread

Read the notes on the soya bean on page 8 to learn more about this wonderful protein food.

The spread is very simple to make and a nutritious base for thickening sauces and soups. It can be added to breakfast cereals such as porridge or semolina as a protein booster or served as a starter with a variety of fresh chopped vegetables, herbs and seasoning.

For instructions on how to sprout the beans, turn to the recipe for Sprouted Soya Bean Soup on page 19. Follow directions 1 and 2, which will tell you how to sprout and cook your beans.

When cooked, purée the beans using *steel blades* with a little sea salt and just enough of the cooking water to achieve a thick creamy consistency.

Sprouted Soya Bean Starter

Imperial (Metric)	American
I recipe Soya Bean Spread (see page 30)	I recipe Soya Bean Spread (see page 30)
¼ cucumber, diced	¼ cucumber, diced
I bunch radishes, sliced	I bunch radishes, sliced
2 tablespoons each chopped red and green peppers	2 tablespoons each chopped red and green peppers
6 spring onions, thinly chopped (use green)	6 scallions, thinly chopped (use green)

To garnish:

Imperial (Metric)	American
I mango *or* 2 medium peaches, skinned and chopped	I mango *or* 2 medium peaches, skinned and chopped
I teaspoon freshly grated ginger root	I teaspoon freshly grated ginger root
I teaspoon clear honey	I teaspoon clear honey
I dessertspoon shoyu (naturally fermented soya sauce)	2 teaspoons naturally fermented soy sauce
I tablespoon lemon juice	I tablespoon lemon juice

1 Place soya bean spread in a serving bowl. Stir in the chopped vegetables.

2 Set *steel blades* in position. Put chopped mango or peaches into the processor bowl. Add the ginger, honey and shoyu (soy sauce) and lemon juice. Blend until smooth. Scoop out.

3 Pour the mango purée over the spread and vegetable mixture. Stir in just before serving. Absolutely delicious.

Note: To make a satisfying lunch, fill pitta bread (see page 161 for recipe) with this wholesome mixture.

Toasted Nut and Seed Pâté

You can use a variety of nuts and seeds for this, some of which are much more expensive than others. For every day I would use a mixture of sunflower seeds, sesame seeds, peanuts or cashews and hazelnuts. My choice in the recipe is great for buffet parties or a special lunch.

Imperial (Metric)	American
12 oz (340g) mixed nuts and seeds (almonds, hazelnuts, cashews, pumpkin seeds and sesame seeds)	2¼ cups mixed nuts and seeds (almonds, hazelnuts, cashews, pumpkin seeds and sesame seeds)
6 tablespoons cold-pressed sunflower oil	6 tablespoons cold-pressed sunflower oil
1 small onion, peeled and roughly chopped	1 small onion, peeled and roughly chopped
½ small red and ½ small green pepper	½ small red and ½ small green pepper
1 tablespoon shoyu (naturally fermented soya sauce)	1 tablespoon naturally fermented soy sauce
1 teaspoon *sweet* mixed herbs	1 teaspoon sweet mixed herbs
¼ pint (140ml) thick natural yogurt	½ cup thick plain yogurt
Freshly ground black pepper to taste	Freshly ground black pepper to taste

1 Toast the nuts and seeds in a heavy-based pan on moderate heat, turning constantly with a wooden spoon until lightly roasted. (Approx. 10 minutes.)

2 Set *steel blades* in position and blend the nuts and seeds in two stages with the cold-pressed oil until nearly smooth. (The texture is up to you, the longer you process the smoother the pâté.) Scoop out and place in a serving bowl.

3 Put onion, red and green pepper, shoyu (soy sauce) and mixed herbs into the processor bowl and blend until puréed.

4 Stir the purée, with the yogurt, into the ground nuts and seeds. Taste and add freshly ground black pepper and a little more shoyu (soy sauce) if you wish.

Note: Delicious as a dip, wonderful in my recipe for Stuffed Courgettes (see page 119) and a nutritious and tasty sandwich filler.

Hummous

This section would not be complete without this beautiful purée which originates from the Middle East.

Imperial (Metric)	American
8 oz (225g) chick peas, dry weight	I cup dry garbanzo beans
Juice of 2 lemons	Juice of 2 lemons
2 large cloves of garlic	2 large cloves of garlic
2 tablespoons tahini (sesame seed paste)	2 tablespoons tahini (sesame seed paste)
2 tablespoons olive oil	2 tablespoons olive oil
Sea salt and freshly ground black pepper	Sea salt and freshly ground black pepper
Mint to garnish	Mint to garnish

1 Wash the peas (beans) well, picking over for stones.

2 Soak peas (beans) for at least 12 hours, changing the water three times. Rinse and cook in 2 pints (5 cups) water for 1 hour or until soft. Add 1 tablespoon sea salt 10 minutes before end of cooking time.

3 Set *steel blades* in position. Put half the peas (beans) into the processor bowl with half of all the other ingredients. Blend until smooth. (You might have to add a little cooking water, but only enough to achieve a thick creamy consistency.) Scoop out.

4 Now put the other half of all the ingredients into the processor bowl. Blend as before until smooth, adding cooking water if necessary.

5 Place in a serving bowl. Add sea salt and freshly ground black pepper to taste. Garnish with a sprig of mint.

Timbales

Although the recipes that follow originate from Mediterranean cuisine, they were first introduced to me by Colin Spencer, a fantastic vegetarian cookery writer for whom I have great respect. Every cook has their own way of preparing similar dishes, but the stimulus is exciting when you find it.

A timbale is traditionally cooked in a dish of the same name which has sloping sides. It is then turned out much like you would turn out a jelly, sliced and served with an accompanying sauce. Well, I find them delicious enough on their own, cooked in ramekins, as a light and tasty starter. Basically they are a variety of savoury egg custard which is steam-baked in the oven.

I will give you the recipe for my favourite timbale and suggest others that I'm sure will delight your palate. All the recipes fit four large ramekins or six average size.

Asparagus Timbale

Imperial (Metric)	American
8 oz (225g) frozen or fresh asparagus	8 ounces frozen or fresh asparagus
3 tablespoons single cream	3 tablespoons light cream
1 very level teaspoon tarragon	1 very level teaspoon tarragon
¼ teaspoon mustard powder	¼ teaspoon mustard powder
¼ teaspoon ground mace	¼ teaspoon ground mace
½ teaspoon sea salt	½ teaspoon sea salt
½ teaspoon freshly ground black pepper	½ teaspoon freshly ground black pepper
4 standard eggs	4 standard eggs
3 oz (85g) grated farmhouse Cheddar cheese	¾ cup grated Cheddar cheese
8 fl oz (230ml) milk	1 cup milk

1 If using frozen asparagus, then just steam for 10 minutes. If fresh, cut off woody parts from base. Scrape the white parts of the stems downwards. Tie up in a bundle, immerse in boiling water to just below the tips and boil for 12 to 15 minutes.

2 Cut off the very tips and put to one side, covered, in a dish.

3 Chop the stems into 1 inch (2.5cm) pieces. Cool. Set *steel blades* in position. Place the asparagus stems, cream and tarragon in the processor bowl. Blend until smooth. Scoop out into a bowl.

4 Add mustard, mace, sea salt and pepper.

5 Whisk eggs and beat into the asparagus mixture.

6 Stir in the grated cheese.

7 Warm the milk and pour this gradually into the egg mixture, beating continuously as you do so.

8 Grease the ramekins well and pour the mixture into these, taking care not to overfill.

9 Pop a few asparagus tips into each ramekin. Place the ramekins on a baking tray in which you have put some boiling water. Bake on lowest shelf in the oven at 350°F/170°C (Gas Mark 4) for 40 minutes.

Variations:

Leek Timbale

Use exactly the same ingredients, but substitute 8 oz (225g) leeks (weight when trimmed and washed) for the asparagus.

1 Trim leeks by cutting an indent around the area where the coarse green starts. Underneath the coarse leaves you will find some tender green ones: leave them attached. Wash leeks and chop into approx. ¾ inch (2 cm) pieces.

2 Sauté the leeks in 2 tablespoons olive or sunflower oil for 10 minutes on low heat with lid on the pan. Cool.

3 Set *steel blades* in position and purée the leeks with the cream and tarragon until smooth.

4 Proceed as for asparagus timbale. Sprinkle a very little dried tarragon on top just before baking.

Broccoli Timbale

For this recipe I sometimes use 3 oz (85g) of firm goat's cheese which crumbles or breaks easily. I substitute 4 broccoli spears for the asparagus and use basil and chopped chives, or the green ends of spring onions (scallions) if no chives are available, instead of tarragon. A *very little* garlic is also a delicious addition — about half a medium-sized clove, crushed.

1 Steam the broccoli spears for 15 minutes until soft.

2 Chop and let cool.

3 Set *steel blades* in position. Put chopped broccoli, the crumbled goat's cheese, cream, 1 teaspoon basil, 1 tablespoon chopped chives and the crushed garlic into the processor bowl. Blend until smooth.

4 Proceed as for asparagus timbale.

Mushroom Timbale

Instead of using the cream and the Cheddar cheese I use 5 oz (140g) yogurt cheese. To make this you will need to strain ½ large carton of natural yogurt, approximately 10 ounces (285g) in weight, through a piece of muslin to get 5 ounces (140g) when dripped overnight. I substitute mushroom for the asparagus, add 1 teaspoon crushed coriander seeds and leave out the tarragon. I also sprinkle the tops with a little Parmesan cheese just before baking.

1 Wash and towel dry 6 oz (170g) mushrooms. Sauté whole with the ground coriander seeds in a covered pan until soft. Drain in a sieve. Let cool.

2 Set *steel blades* in position. Blend the mushrooms with the yogurt cheese until smooth.

3 Proceed as with asparagus timbale, but sprinkle the tops with a little grated Parmesan cheese just before baking.

2.

MAIN MEALS

I think a fitting beginning to this chapter is to give you a foolproof recipe for making tofu (soya cheese). It is a most nutritious, high-protein food, very cheap to produce and the wholesome core of a well-balanced vegetarian diet.

The recipes that follow will include dried peas and beans, wholegrains, nuts and seeds and that much maligned technological masterpiece tvp (texturized vegetable protein). For more information on this wonderful innovation turn to page 38.

Because of the huge variety of foods used in vegetarian wholefood cuisine the recipes span the globe, which makes cooking an exciting experience rather than a mundane chore. I would definitely not be writing cookbooks today if I had not been introduced to wholefoods a few years ago. I have learnt so much about the way other people live through reading about their eating habits. So my main meals will give you a taste of many lands, including the Mediterranean countries, the Middle East, India, Japan and South America.

You will find your processor invaluable for chopping the many vegetables included in the recipes and marvellous for making savoury batters and pancakes.

Pulses and Tvp

Dried peas, beans and lentils provide a good cheap source of protein, ranging from 17 per cent to 25 per cent, except for the soya bean which is approximately 38 per cent protein, equal to that of meat.

The protein in these pulses used to be considered 'second class', which is understandable because only the soya bean contains all the essential amino acids needed by the body to build protein. However, through research scientists have found that pulses used in combination with other foods which have the missing proteins will provide a complete protein with all the amino acids in balance.

This all sounds very complicated but it is really quite simple. The missing proteins in pulses are to be found in wholegrains, nuts and seeds and dairy produce. The right combinations go so well together that this balancing is often instinctive, and this is apparent in Eastern and Middle Eastern cuisine as well as that of South America. In fact, people all over the world have united the right protein foods without ever reading a cookbook, not to mention scientific reports. It is sad to realize that we in the West, and to some extent all over the globe, are in grave danger of losing our natural instincts regarding nature's whole food because of the increasing tendency to process and refine it.

All raw peas and beans, fresh and dried, contain substances which are harmful to the digestion. Boiling fresh peas and beans for just 10 minutes renders these substances harmless. Proper soaking and cooking of the dried variety will prevent any adverse effects.

It is best to soak the dried peas or beans overnight, changing the water three times. Bring them to boil in fresh water, let boil for 10 minutes, then turn down to simmer and cook until soft. I have given clear directions for soaking and cooking times in the individual recipes, but these times can vary depending on how old the beans are. Cook until soft and do not add salt until 10 minutes before the end of cooking time, otherwise the beans will stay tough.

One more useful tip. Cook more beans than you need and freeze some. They freeze very well. All you do is drain them, put into a plastic container and freeze. They will defrost in 1 hour.

Some of the recipes contain tvp (Texturized Vegetable Protein), which is so often misused. Just 5 ounces (115g) of reconstituted tvp will give you the same amount of protein contained in one pound (445g) of lean beef at a quarter of the price. It's a wonderful food and delicious when used with discretion and the right seasoning, and of course it is cholesterol free.

To Make Soya Milk and Tofu (Soya Cheese)

Read all the instructions carefully and have everything ready before you start.

You can make tofu with Epsom salts or lemon juice, but I find the best results, a higher yield and greater firmness, are achievd by using Nigari. Nigari is rich in minerals and is the residue left after the salt (sodium chloride) and water are removed from sea water. The residue is sun-dried and bought as crystals. I also use a Japanese tofu press which is made from Japanese cypress wood (iroki). The press comes with a sachet of Nigari and full instructions, but it is best to follow my instructions as they give you the exact amount of water to use, which is most important. The quantities given make 1 lb (450g/2 cups) of firm tofu.

Imperial (Metric)	American
12 oz (350g) dry weight soya beans	1½ cups dry soy beans
2 teaspoons (10ml) Nigari, dissolved in 1 cup (200ml) of warm water *or*	2 teaspoons Nigari, dissolved in 1 teacup (200ml) of warm water *or*
3 teaspoons (15ml) Epsom salts, dissolved in 1 teacup of warm water *or*	3 teaspoons Epsom salts, dissolved in 1 teacup of warm water *or*
6 tablespoons (90ml) lemon juice in 1 teacup of warm water (this will give you a tangy, slightly coarse tofu, quite tasty)	6 tablespoons lemon juice in 1 teacup of warm water (this will give you a tangy, slightly coarse tofu, quite tasty)

For the soya milk:

1 Wash and soak the soya beans for 24 hours. Change the water three times during soaking. Rinse the beans well after soaking and to each cup of soaked beans add 1 cup of boiling water and process using *steel blades* cup by cup. Leave the motor on for 1½ minutes each time to achieve a reasonably smooth, runny batter consistency.

2 Grease a heavy-bottomed pan big enough to take about 10 pints (5 litres/25 cups) of liquid. Bring 4 pints (2.3 litres/10 cups) of fresh water to the boil and pour in the liquidized bean purée. Bring to the boil, stirring constantly. Keep on a moderate heat only, to prevent burning. Once boiling, turn down the heat and leave to simmer for 20 minutes. The mixture will be frothy, so spoon back some of the froth to make sure that the liquid is gently bubbling underneath. Stir occasionally.

3 Dissolve the Nigari (or the Epsom salts or lemon juice) in the water to make the solidifier. Stretch a straining bag or good-sized piece of muslin over a colander, leaving plenty for tying up.

4 Place the colander over a large clean bowl to catch the milk. Put on rubber gloves and pour the boiled bean liquid into the straining bag or muslin. The soya milk will filter through. Rinse the cooking pot with 1 cup of boiling water and add this to the straining bag.

5 Twist the bag or cloth tightly and squeeze out as much milk as possible. Open the bag and pour in three more cups of boiling water, tie up and squeeze again.

6 The soya milk is now ready. The milk will freeze well after it is cooled. The quicker you cool the milk, the longer it will keep, so if you don't want to make tofu, cool it by immersing the bowl in a sink of cold water, changing the water as it warms. Soya milk will keep fresh in the refrigerator for up to 4 days. Frozen, it will be good for 3 months at least. You can use soya milk in any recipe requiring cows' milk, especially in sauces.

To make the tofu:

1 Rinse out the cooking pot, pour the hot soya milk back into it and reheat. The milk must reach at least 185°F/85°C, so bring it to just under boiling point. (*Note:* If using Epsom salts, 165°F/64°C is hot enough.) After heating, remove from the cooker and add the chosen solidifier by stirring briskly and *slowly* pouring in one-third of the Nigari, Epsom salts or lemon juice liquid.

2 Continue to stir for half a minute, making sure you stir in milk from the sides and bottom of the pan. Let the movement of the liquid stop then using the back of your stirring spoon, pour a further third of the solidifier on to the surface of the milk. *Cover* and leave for 3 minutes, then stir again.

3 Using the back of the spoon trickle the remaining solidifier over the surface of the milk, then slowly and gently stir only ½ inch (about 1 cm) on the surface of the milk as you count up to 20.

4 Cover and leave for another 3 minutes, then uncover and stir the liquid. You should now have a mixture of curds and whey. The curds will be cream-coloured and the whey a clear yellow colour.

5 Line the tofu press with a clean piece of muslin, draping it over the edge as it will be folded over the tofu later. If you have no press just place the cloth over a colander which is on top of a bowl, to catch the whey. Ladle the curds and whey into the press or colander. The curds will stay in the cloth and the whey will drip through. The tofu will be quite soft at this stage.

6 Fold the cloth over the tofu, place the lid of the press on top (or a small plate if you are using a colander) and a weight on top of this. The weight should be about 2 pounds (1 kilo). Leave to stand for 20-30 minutes. This will give you a firm tofu which is easy to slice.

7 To keep in the refrigerator, fill a bowl with cold water and ease the unwrapped tofu into this. Change the water every day and it will last in the fridge for 6 days. You can freeze it but the texture alters and it is then only good for soups and stews.

Note: Tofu is available commercially in vacuum packs weighing 10½ oz (297g), but this is soft and not easy to use in recipes. You can press it and leave it to drip, which will make it firmer, but you will end up with a very small amount of tofu, so it is not worth while. Although it seems a lengthy process, home-made tofu is well worth the effort.

What to do with the pulp left over after making the soya milk? This is known as *okara*. It is 3.5 per cent protein and is a good fibre to add to your breakfast cereal. It can also be stored.

Recipes Using Tofu

Simple Sautéd Tofu

I usually sauté tofu before adding it to any stir-fried vegetables with an accompanying sauce or add it to vegetable soups if I wish to make a more substantial protein meal.

Imperial (Metric)	American
½ lb (225g) firm pressed tofu	I cup firm pressed tofu
Shoyu (naturally fermented soya sauce)	Naturally fermented soy sauce
2 oz (55g) wholemeal flour	½ cup wholewheat flour
Garlic salt and freshly ground black pepper	Garlic salt and freshly ground black pepper
I teaspoon oregano *or* sweet mixed herbs	I teaspoon oregano *or* sweet mixed herbs
Sunflower *or* sesame seed oil for frying	Sunflower *or* sesame seed oil for frying

1 Cut the tofu into ¾ inch (2cm) cubes. Place in a dish. Sprinkle shoyu over these. Let stand for a few minutes.

2 Mix flour, garlic salt, pepper and herbs in a small bowl.

3 Coat the cubes of tofu in the flour mixture.

4 Put ¼ inch (0.6cm) oil in the pan (sesame oil is superb but very expensive). Heat the oil and fry the tofu, turning it on all sides until golden-brown.

Sweet and Sour Tofu
Serves 4

This is a refreshing, delicious and authentic tasting Chinese meal. The sauce is easy to prepare and a complement to the blander taste of tofu. I serve it with fried rice or just plain boiled rice and a seasonal salad. I also use sesame seed oil because of its wonderful flavour, but sunflower oil will do. I use turnip, which I find is a good substitute for bamboo shoot and much cheaper.

Imperial (Metric)	American
I medium carrot, scraped	I medium carrot, scraped
I small turnip, thinly peeled	I small turnip, thinly peeled
I small to medium onion, peeled	I small to medium onion, peeled
I small green *or* red pepper, de-seeded	I small green *or* red pepper, de-seeded
3 tablespoons sesame or sunflower oil	3 tablespoons sesame or sunflower oil
I clove garlic, peeled and crushed	I clove garlic, peeled and crushed
I level teaspoon fresh ginger root, grated	I level teaspoon fresh ginger root, grated
½ teaspoon five spice powder *or* allspice	½ teaspoon five spice powder *or* allspice
4 oz (115g) pineapple (fresh or tinned), crushed	4 ounces pineapple (fresh or canned), crushed
2 tablespoons soft brown sugar	2 tablespoons soft brown sugar
3 tablespoons cider vinegar	3 tablespoons cider vinegar
2 tablespoons shoyu (naturally fermented soya sauce)	2 tablespoons naturally fermented soy sauce
2 tablespoons tomato purée	2 tablespoons tomato paste
I tablespoon arrowroot	I tablespoon arrowroot
8 fl oz (225ml) water	I cup water

1 Set *slicing plate* in position. Cut carrot widthwise in half, stand these upright in the feed tube and cut into rings.

2 Cut turnip in quarters. Place 2 quarters at a time standing upright in the feed tube and slice.

3 Cut onion in half and place one half at a time in the feed tube. Slice.

4 Flatten the pepper slightly and pack into the feed tube standing upright. Slice. Exert more pressure on the pusher to get thickish slices of pepper.

5 Heat oil in a pan or wok and sauté the carrot, turnip and garlic for 3 minutes only on moderately high heat.

6 Add the onion and pepper and continue to fry for 3 minutes only.

7 Stir in ginger, ground five spice and pineapple. Take off heat.

8 Mix all the other ingredients together, gradually adding the water as you would to make a batter.

9 Pour this over the vegetables. If too thick add a little more water, if a little runny just mix one teaspoon arrowroot with a little water and stir in. Let cook until it thickens. Serve with Toasted Almond Rice, see page 76 for recipe, and a fresh salad.

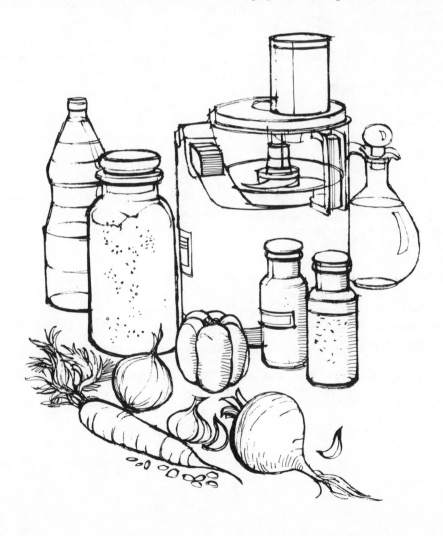

Tofu Tempura

Tempura is the Middle Eastern name for deep fried battered vegetables (see page 92 for Vegetable Tempura). In India it is called Pakora. The batter can be made with wholemeal flour but I prefer the delicate taste of gram — chick pea (garbanzo) flour — which makes a mouth-watering and crisp batter.

This recipe goes very well with stir-fried vegetables, Sweet and Sour Sauce (page 42) and fried rice.

Imperial (Metric)	American
For the batter:	
4 oz (115g) gram flour	4 ounces gram flour
½ teaspoon sea salt	½ teaspoon sea salt
½ level teaspoon baking powder (crispens the batter)	½ level teaspoon baking powder (crispens the batter)
6 fl oz (170ml) cold water	¾ cup cold water
12 oz (340g) firm tofu	1½ cups firm tofu
Shoyu (naturally fermented soya sauce)	Naturally fermented soy sauce
A little wholemeal flour for coating	A little wholewheat flour for coating
Soya oil for deep frying	Soya oil for deep frying

1 With *steel blades* in position, put gram flour, sea salt and baking powder into the processor bowl with half the water. Process until smooth, gradually pouring in the rest of the water through the feed tube with the motor on. Blend until smooth. Let stand for 30 minutes.

2 Cut the tofu into 1 inch (2.5cm) cubes. Sprinkle with shoyu (soy sauce). Let stand for 5 minutes. When the batter is ready, roll the cubes in the flour and dip into the batter. The best way is to settle a cube in the curve of the fork, dip into the batter and the excess batter will trickle through the prongs. Deep fry in hot oil until golden.

3 If using a sweet and sour sauce, then make the sauce first (page 42) and cook the tempura just before serving.

Soya Bean Burgers
Makes 8

These go down well with Spiced Tomato Sauce (page 69).

Imperial (Metric)	American
6 oz (185g) dry weight soya beans	¾ cup dry soy beans
3 oz (115g) porridge oats	¾ cup rolled oats
I medium onion	I medium onion
I clove garlic, crushed	I clove garlic, crushed
I small red or green pepper	I small red or green pepper
Few sprigs of parsley	Few sprigs of parsley
I tablespoon shoyu (naturally fermented soya sauce)	I tablespoon naturally fermented soy sauce
I teaspoon basil	I teaspoon basil
I tablespoon lemon juice	I tablespoon lemon juice
I tablespoon olive oil	I tablespoon olive oil
I egg	I egg
Freshly ground black pepper	Freshly ground black pepper
Oil for frying	Oil for frying

1 Soak and cook soya beans as directed in the Soya Bean Loaf recipe on page 47. Drain.

2 Set *shredding plate* in position and pack beans into the feed tube; process until all the beans are grated. Put into a mixing bowl.

3 Add the porridge oats.

4 Set *steel blades* in position. Chop onion and garlic roughly. Chop pepper in chunks. Place with the parsley in the processor bowl. Chop.

5 Scoop out and add with the shoyu (soy sauce), basil, lemon juice, one tablespoon olive oil and the egg to the bean and oat mixture. Mould well together. Add freshly ground black pepper to taste.

6 Form into balls slightly bigger than a golf ball. Flatten to ½ inch (1.5cm) deep.

7 Fry in hot oil ¼ inch (0.6cm) deep, turning to brown on both sides: approximately 3 minutes on each side, so use moderate heat.

Red Bean Chilli Stew
Serves 4

This is a Mexican dish which is usually made with beef and red kidney beans. I have used tvp (texturized vegetable protein), beef flavoured, with very good results, according to my family and students. See note on tvp on page 38. The beef flavouring is an extract of soya and is completely natural.

Imperial (Metric)	American
8 oz (225g) red kidney beans	I cup red kidney beans
I level teaspoon sea salt	I level teaspoon sea salt
I teaspoon honey	I teaspoon honey
2½ oz (70g) tvp mince, beef flavoured	2½ ounces tvp mince, beef flavoured
I tablespoon shoyu (naturally fermented soya sauce)	I tablespoon naturally fermented soy sauce
I large onion, cut in quarters lengthwise	I large onion, cut in quarters lengthwise
I medium green pepper, de-seeded and cut quarters in lengthwise	I medium green pepper, de-seeded and cut in quarters lengthwise
4 oz (115g) mushrooms (optional, but nice)	2 cups mushrooms (optional, but nice)
2 tablespoons sunflower oil	2 tablespoons sunflower oil
14 oz (395g) tinned tomatoes, chopped	14 ounces canned tomatoes, chopped
I very level teaspoon crushed cumin seed	I very level teaspoon crushed cumin seed
I-2 level teaspoons chilli powder	I-2 level teaspoons chili powder
Sea salt, to taste	Sea salt, to taste

1 Wash beans and pick over for stones. Soak for 12 hours. Change the water 3 times.

2 Bring to boil in fresh cold water. Boil for 10 minutes and simmer for 40 minutes more. Add salt and honey 10 minutes before end of cooking time. (Check the beans because they can get very mushy.) Drain.

3 Reconstitute the soya mince in its same volume of boiling water plus the shoyu (soy sauce) for 10 minutes to swell and absorb all the liquid.

4 Set *slicing plate* in position. Stand onion in an upright position in the tube and slice. Scoop out. Slice peppers, standing these upright, and then the mushrooms, caps facing the outside of the feed tube.

5 Heat oil in a pan. Sauté the onion for 5 minutes, with a lid on the pan. Add the soya mince and continue to fry for 4 minutes.

6 Add the peppers and mushrooms and continue to fry for 3 minutes more. Stir in the beans.

7 Add tomatoes, ground cumin seeds and chilli powder, and stir well together. Taste and add sea salt if necessary. Simmer on very low heat, so that the flavour soaks into the beans, for 25 minutes. Do not burn, and keep a tight lid on. You can bake in the oven at 325°F/160°C (Gas Mark 3) for 30 minutes in a tightly-covered casserole dish. Serve in individual dishes with rice and a small bowl of thick yogurt and cucumber salad.

Soya Bean and Bulgur Loaf
Serves 4

This is a high-protein meal. Bulgur is a wheat product which is sold parboiled and only needs soaking before use. The wheatgerm and bran remain intact. You will find more recipes using bulgur in the section on wholegrains, page 66, and as a salad, Tabbouleh, page 110. The loaf is lovely hot or cold.

Imperial (Metric)	American
6 oz (170g) dry weight soya beans	¾ cup dry soya beans
2 oz (55g) bulgur wheat	⅓ cup bulgur wheat
1½ tablespoons shoyu (naturally fermented soya sauce)	1½ tablespoons naturally fermented soy sauce
1 large onion, peeled	1 large onion, peeled
4 oz (115g) mushrooms	2 cups mushrooms
3 tablespoons sunflower oil	3 tablespoons sunflower oil
1 large clove garlic, peeled and crushed	1 large clove garlic, peeled and crushed
2 tablespoons lemon juice	2 tablespoons lemon juice
3 tablespoons fresh chopped parsley	3 tablespoons fresh chopped parsley
1 egg	1 egg
Freshly ground black pepper	Freshly ground black pepper
Extra bulgur wheat and oil for loaf tin	Extra bulgur wheat and oil for loaf tin

1 Wash beans and soak for 24 hours, changing the water three times. Rinse and cook for at least 3 hours until soft. Drain.

2 Soak bulgur in enough boiling water plus 2 teaspoons shoyu (soy sauce) to cover it by ½ inch (1.5cm) for 20 minutes.

3 Set *shredding plate* in position. Put beans into the feed tube, pack in well, and

process until all the beans are grated. Put into a mixing bowl. Add the soaked bulgur, and mix together.

4 Set *slicing plate* in position. Cut onion in quarters lengthwise, pack into the feed tube and slice. Scoop out.

5 Wash and wipe mushrooms. Slice in the same way.

6 Heat oil in a pan. Sauté the onion and garlic, covered, for 7 minutes until soft. Stir into beans.

7 Sauté the mushrooms for 2 minutes only. Stir in the lemon juice, remaining shoyu (soy sauce), parsley and freshly ground black pepper.

8 Stir this into the beans. Mix well. Break in the egg and mould mixture together with your hands.

9 Grease a 1 pound (500g) loaf tin and sprinkle on a little bulgur wheat. Put loaf mixture into this. Trickle a little oil over the top, cover with foil and bake for 1 hour at 375°F/190°C (Gas Mark 5).

10 Turn out on a serving dish. Delicious with Spiced Tomato Sauce, see page 69 for recipe, baked jacket potatoes and lightly steamed broccoli.

Borlotti Bean Shepherd's Pie
Serves 4

Imperial (Metric)	American
6 oz (170g) Borlotti beans, dry weight	I cup dry Borlotti beans
2 large carrots, scraped	2 large carrots, scraped
I large onion, peeled	I large onion, peeled
3 tablespoons sunflower oil	3 tablespoons sunflower oil
4 tomatoes	4 tomatoes
I vegetable stock cube dissolved in ⅓ pint (200ml) hot water	I vegetable stock cube dissolved in ¾ cup hot water
2 tablespoons parsley, roughly chopped	2 tablespoons parsley, roughly chopped
I level teaspoon marjoram	I level teaspoon marjoram
Freshly ground black pepper	Freshly ground black pepper

For the topping:

Imperial (Metric)	American
2 lbs (1.1 kilos) potatoes, steamed	2 pounds potatoes, steamed
1 oz (30g) polyunsaturated margarine	2 tablespoons polyunsaturated margarine
2 tablespoons thick natural yogurt	2 tablespoons thick plain yogurt
Sea salt and freshly ground black pepper	Sea salt and freshly ground black pepper
3 oz (85g) grated Cheddar cheese	¾ cup grated Cheddar cheese

1 Wash and soak the beans for at least 8 hours. Change the water three times. Rinse and boil in fresh water for 10 minutes. Let simmer for 40 minutes more. Drain, put into a baking dish and mash.

2 Slice carrots lengthwise so that you have 4 long thin sticks. Then cut in half widthwise. Cut onion lengthwise in half or in quarters to fit feed tube snugly.

3 Set *slicing plate* in position. Pack the carrot fingers tightly, in an upright position into the feed tube. Slice. Pack onion into the feed tube and slice.

4 Heat oil in a pan. Sauté the carrot and onion for 10 minutes, with the lid on, until soft. Fork into the mashed beans.

5 Skin the tomatoes by cutting a circle around the stalk and blanch in boiling water for 5 minutes. The skins will come away easily.

6 Set *steel blades* in position. Pour in the hot stock, parsley, marjoram, pepper and the skinned tomatoes. Blend until smooth. Fork into the bean mixture.

7 Set *shredding plate* in position. Peel off skins from the steamed potatoes. (If new leave skins on.) Roughly chop potatoes into 1½ inch (3cm) pieces. Pack into the feed tube and process. Scoop out. Mix in the margarine and yogurt. Season with a little sea salt and freshly ground black pepper.

8 Spread over the bean mixture. Fork pattern the top. Sprinkle on the grated cheese. Bake at 400°F/200°C (Gas Mark 6) for 40 minutes until the top is golden-brown.

Aduki Bean Hot Pot
Serves 4

Aduki beans originate from Japan and China and are widely used there still. A very meaty tasting bean, easy to digest and quick to cook. This recipe is always popular, even with those new to bean cuisine. I use tvp (textured vegetable protein) beef flavour as it goes very well with beans and tomatoes. (See note on tvp on page 38.) You can use mung beans (small green beans which cook in the same way as aduki beans).

Imperial (Metric)	American
5 oz (140g) dry weight aduki beans	⅔ cup dry aduki beans
Level teaspoon sea salt	Level teaspoon sea salt
2 oz (55g) beef flavoured tvp	2 ounces beef flavoured tvp
I large onion, peeled	I large onion, peeled
A few sprigs parsley	A few sprigs parsley
2 medium carrots, scraped	2 medium carrots, scraped
2 sticks celery	2 stalks celery
3 tablespoons sunflower oil	3 tablespoons sunflower oil
I teaspoon basil	I teaspoon basil
I bay leaf	I bay leaf
14 oz (395g) tin tomatoes, chopped	14 ounces canned tomatoes, chopped
I tablespoon tomato purée	I tablespoon tomato paste
I tablespoon shoyu	I tablespoon soy sauce

For the topping:

Imperial (Metric)	American
1½ - 2 lbs (680-900g) potatoes, scrubbed and steamed for 15 minutes	1½ to 2 pounds potatoes, scrubbed and steamed for 15 minutes
2 oz (55g) grated Cheddar cheese	½ cup grated Cheddar cheese
A little basil	A little basil

1 Wash beans and pick over for stones. Soak for 5 hours. Change water after one hour.

2 Rinse and cook beans in fresh water. Cook for 35 minutes until soft. Add just under a level teaspoon sea salt just before end of cooking time. Place cooked beans and 7 fl oz (200ml/¾ cup) cooking water in an ovenproof baking dish.

3 Soak tvp in its same volume of boiling water. Leave for 10 minutes when it will have absorbed all the water.

4 Set *steel blades* in position. Chop onion in chunks, chop parsley, chop carrot lengthwise, then into approximately ¾ inch (2cm) pieces, chop celery in ¾ inch (2cm) pieces. Place all in the processor bowl. Chop finely.

5 Heat oil in the pan. Sauté the chopped vegetables with the soaked tvp, basil and bay leaf for 5 minutes. Stir in the chopped tomatoes, purée and shoyu (soy sauce). Bring to boil. Stir a few times and pour into the beans. The mixture will be runny but it dries a little with cooking.

6 Slice the steamed potatoes thinly (they should still be firm). Place slices overlapping on top of the bean mixture. Sprinkle on the grated cheese and a little basil.

7 Bake at 375°F/190°C (Gas Mark 5) for 30 minutes. Then turn up heat to 425°/220°C (Gas Mark 7). Bake for another 10 minutes or until brown on top.

Black-eye Bean and Aubergine (Eggplant) Moussaka
Serves 4

The aubergine or eggplant is a staple vegetable of the Middle East. It is the main ingredient in Moussaka. Minced beef or lamb are often added, so I have substituted black-eye beans which have a savoury nutty flavour and are soft-skinned so absorb other flavours easily. Red kidney beans also go extremely well with aubergines (eggplant). It is a rich dish, just right for a special dinner party. I add a glass of red wine to the liquid when entertaining, instead of the water.

Imperial (Metric)	American
8 oz (225g) black-eye beans, dry weight	I cup dry black-eye beans
I level teaspoon sea salt	I level teaspoon sea salt
3 aubergines, approx. 8 oz (225g) each in weight	3 eggplants, approx. 8 ounces each in weight
4 large tomatoes	4 large tomatoes
I tablespoon tomato purée	I tablespoon tomato paste
¼ pint (140ml) hot water	⅔ cup hot water
½ vegetable stock cube	½ vegetable stock cube
2 medium onions, peeled and cut in half lengthwise	2 medium onions, peeled and cut in half lengthwise
6 tablespoons olive oil	6 tablespoons olive oil
Freshly ground black pepper	Freshly ground black pepper

For the topping:

Imperial (Metric)	American
I rounded tablespoon gram flour (chick pea flour)	I rounded tablespoon gram flour (garbanzo bean flour)
I rounded tablespoon 81 per cent wheatmeal flour	I rounded tablespoon 81 per cent wheatmeal flour
I egg	I egg
8 fl oz (225ml) milk	I cup milk
3 tablespoons thick natural yogurt	3 tablespoons thick plain yogurt
Sea salt and freshly ground black pepper	Sea salt and freshly ground black pepper

1 Wash beans and soak for at least 8 hours. Change water three times.

2 Bring to boil in fresh water. Let boil for 10 minutes then simmer for 40 minutes more or until soft. Add a little sea salt 10 minutes before end of cooking time. Drain and set aside.

3 Wash and thinly slice the aubergines (eggplants). Arrange them in layers in a colander. Sprinkle each layer with sea salt. Let stand for 30 minutes. (This process draws off bitter juices.)

4 Meanwhile skin the tomatoes by cutting a circle around the stalk end. Blanch in boiling water for 5 minutes. Peel off skins.

5 Set *steel blades* in position. Put tomatoes, tomato purée (paste) and the hot water, in which you have dissolved the ½ stock cube, into the processor bowl. Blend until smooth. Pour into a jug. Rinse out the processor bowl and wipe dry.

6 Set *slicing plate* in position. Slice onion a half at a time (stand upright in the feed tube).

7 Heat 2 tablespoons olive oil in a pan. Sauté the onion, covered, for 7 minutes until soft.

8 Stir in the beans and the tomato stock liquid, add freshly ground black pepper and cook gently with a lid on for 10 minutes.

9 Rinse aubergine (eggplant) slices and pat dry on absorbent kitchen paper. Sauté in the remaining 4 tablespoons olive oil until golden.

10 Oil a large ovenproof baking dish. Arrange a layer of aubergines (eggplants), and the oil you cooked them in, on the bottom. Spoon a layer of the bean mixture over these, then another layer of aubergines (eggplants) and so on, finishing up with a layer of aubergines (eggplants).

For the topping:

1 With the *steel blades* in position, place the gram flour, wheatmeal flour, egg and half the milk into the processor bowl. Blend until smooth. Gradually add the remaining milk through the feed tube while the motor is still on. Finally blend in the yogurt. Season with freshly ground black pepper and sea salt.

2 Pour this batter over the aubergine (eggplant) mixture. Place in the centre of a preheated oven, 350°F/180°C (Gas Mark 4). Bake for 35 to 40 minutes until golden brown and bubbling on the top.

Note: You can sprinkle 3 ounces (85g) of finely grated Cheddar or Parmesan cheese over the top before baking.

Butter Bean Gratin
Serves 4

Imperial (Metric)	American
8 oz (225g) butter beans, dry weight	1⅓ cups dry butter beans
½ teaspoon sea salt	½ teaspoon sea salt
8 oz (225g) broccoli *or* cauliflower florets	8 ounces broccoli *or* cauliflower florets
8 oz (225g) leeks, weight when trimmed and washed	8 ounces leeks, weight when trimmed and washed
¾ pint (425ml) milk and vegetable cooking water (see points 4 and 5)	2 cups milk and vegetable cooking water (see points 4 and 5)
½ level teaspoon ground mace	½ level teaspoon ground mace
½ teaspoon ground mustard	½ teaspoon ground mustard
2 oz (55g) 81 per cent wheatmeal flour	2 ounces 81 per cent wheatmeal flour
4 oz (115g) farmhouse Cheddar cheese, grated	1 cup grated farmhouse Cheddar cheese
Freshly ground black pepper	Freshly ground black pepper

1 Wash and soak the butter beans for at least 8 hours, changing the water 3 times.

2 Boil in fresh water for 10 minutes then simmer for another 50 minutes until soft. Add a little sea salt 10 minutes before end of cooking time. Watch beans because they get very mushy near the end of cooking time. Drain and set aside.

3 Trim broccoli and leeks. Wash well. Leave broccoli in small florets and cut leeks in 1 inch (2cm) pieces.

4 Bring ½ pint (285ml/1¾ cups) water to boil, add ½ teaspoon sea salt. Boil broccoli and leeks for 10 minutes only. They must still be firm. Drain and reserve the liquid.

5 Set *steel blades* in position. Put vegetable cooking water in a measuring jug, add cold milk to the level of ¾ pint (425ml/2 cups). Place in the processor bowl. Add mace, mustard, and flour. Process until well blended.

6 Pour into a heavy-bottomed saucepan. Bring to boil on moderate heat, stirring constantly. Let simmer, still stirring, for 2 minutes. Take off heat.

7 Stir in half the grated cheese. Add sea salt and freshly ground black pepper to taste.

8 To assemble the bake: put half the butter beans in a baking dish. Spoon broccoli or cauliflower florets and leeks on top, then spoon the rest of the beans over these. Pour cheese sauce on top. Sprinkle on the remaining grated cheese.

9 Bake at 400°F/200°C (Gas Mark 6) for 20 minutes. If not brown enough on top put under a grill (broiler) to finish.

Chick Pea (Garbanzo) Falafal
Makes 32

I love these beautiful chick pea balls served with yogurt and salad or, for a real tummy warmer, with hot Spiced Tomato Sauce (see page 69), pitta bread (see page 161) and crisp lettuce.

Imperial (Metric)	American
12 oz (340g) chick peas, dry weight	1⅔ cups dry garbanzo beans
2 oz (55g) bulgur	½ cup bulgur
3 tablespoons olive oil	3 tablespoons olive oil
2 cloves garlic, crushed	2 cloves garlic, crushed
2 level teaspoons tahini (sesame seed paste)	2 level teaspoons tahini (sesame seed paste)
3 tablespoons lemon juice	3 tablespoons lemon juice
½ teaspoon freshly ground black pepper	½ teaspoon freshly ground black pepper
I level teaspoon ground coriander	I level teaspoon ground coriander
I very level teaspoon cayenne pepper (optional)	I very level teaspoon cayenne pepper (optional)
I teaspoon freshly chopped mint (optional)	I teaspoon freshly chopped mint (optional)
Wholemeal flour, to coat	Wholewheat flour, to coat
Soya oil for deep frying	Soy oil for deep frying
Sea salt	Sea salt
Honey	Honey

1 Wash peas (beans) and pick over for stones. Soak for at least 12 hours. Change the water three times. Boil in fresh water for 10 minutes and simmer for approximately 50 minutes to one hour more until soft. Drain. Soak bulgur in enough boiling water to cover by ½ inch (1cm).

2 Set *fine shredding plate* in position. Pack chick peas (garbanzo beans) into the feed tube and grate. The resulting mixture will be powdery flakes. Place in a bowl. Mix all ingredients together, adding salt and honey to taste.

3 Form into walnut size balls. Coat in flour and deep fry in hot oil until golden brown. As suggested, serve with a sauce and a salad of your choice.

Chick Pea (Garbanzo), Tomato and Tarragon Casserole
Serves 4

Imperial (Metric)	American
8 oz (225g) dry weight chick peas	I cup dry garbanzo beans
12 oz (340g) soft ripe tomatoes	12 ounces soft ripe tomatoes
I medium onion, peeled and cut in half lengthwise	I medium onion, peeled and cut in half lengthwise
I large green pepper	I large green pepper
3 tablespoons olive oil	3 tablespoons olive oil
2 cloves garlic, crushed	2 cloves garlic, crushed
I teaspoon ground coriander	I teaspoon ground coriander
I teaspoon basil	I teaspoon basil
I teaspoon dried tarragon, double the amount if fresh	I teaspoon dried tarragon, double the amount if fresh
I tablespoon fresh chopped parsley	I tablespoon fresh chopped parsley
Sea salt and freshly ground black pepper	Sea salt and freshly ground black pepper

1 Wash peas (beans) and pick over carefully for stones. Soak for 12 hours, changing the water 3 times. Bring to boil in fresh cold water. Let boil for 10 minutes then simmer for 50 minutes to one hour more until soft. Drain.

2 Skin the tomatoes by cutting a circle around the edge of the stalk end. Blanch in boiling water for 5 minutes, then peel. Chop well.

3 Set *slicing plate* in position. Slice each half onion, standing them in an upright position in the feed tube. Scoop out. Now cut pepper in quarters and stand upright in the feed tube; slice.

4 Heat oil in a pan. Sauté the onion and garlic for 10 minutes until soft. Cover pan with a lid.

5 Add the peppers, coriander, basil, tarragon and parsley. Continue to sauté for 2 minutes only.

6 Add the chopped tomatoes. Stir well. Taste and add sea salt and freshly ground black pepper to taste.

7 Combine the peas (beans) with the tomato mixture and place in a casserole, cover tightly and bake at 300°F/150°C (Gas Mark 2) for 1½ hours. (You can bake

on a slightly higher temperature for one hour but I prefer them baked this slowly so that the peas absorb the flavour of the sauce.)

8 Delicious stirred into bulgur wheat with a sprinkling of lemon juice and garnished with fresh chopped parsley and mint. Hot or cold it is superb.

Aduki Bean Burgers
Makes 8

These are marvellous for using up any leftover cooked grains such as rice, bulgur or buckwheat. If no cooked grains are available then 3 oz (85g/¾ cup) porridge oats will do.

Imperial (Metric)	American
6 oz (170g) dry weight aduki beans	¾ cup dry aduki beans
Cooked brown rice to reach a level of 8 fl oz (240ml) in a measuring jug	1 cup cooked brown rice
1 medium onion, peeled	1 medium onion, peeled
Few sprigs of parsley	Few sprigs of parsley
Small clove garlic, crushed	Small clove garlic, crushed
1 teaspoon basil	1 teaspoon basil
2 tablespoons tomato purée	2 tablespoons tomato paste
1 tablespoon shoyu	1 tablespoon soy sauce
Freshly ground black pepper	Freshly ground black pepper
1 egg	1 egg
Soya oil for frying	Soy oil for frying

1 Wash and cook the beans as directed in the previous recipe. Drain well. Put in a mixing bowl.

2 Set *steel blades* in position. Process the cooked rice. Scoop out and add to beans.

3 Cut onions into chunks. With steel blades still in position chop onion, parsley and garlic. Scoop out and add to bean mixture.

4 Add basil, tomato purée (paste), shoyu (soy sauce), freshly ground black pepper and the egg to the other ingredients. Mould together and form into burger shapes ½ inch (1 cm) thick. Fry in a little soya oil until lightly browned on both sides (about 3 minutes on each side should be long enough). Serve with onion sauce, mashed potatoes and lightly steamed vegetables. Delicious cold with a fresh salad.

Haricot Beans with Courgettes (Zucchini) and Mushrooms au Gratin

You can use flageolet beans for this recipe if you wish. They are young, dried, pale green beans, which take less time to cook than haricot but they are more expensive. See page 111 for a salad recipe using these delicately flavoured beans.

Imperial (Metric)	American
8 oz (225g) haricot beans, dry weight	I cup dry navy beans
I level teaspoon sea salt	I level teaspoon sea salt
I large onion, cut into quarters lengthwise	I large onion, cut into quarters lengthwise
3 tablespoons olive oil *or* sunflower oil	3 tablespoons olive oil *or* sunflower oil
2 cloves garlic	2 cloves garlic
4 medium courgettes	4 medium zucchini
I medium green pepper, de-seeded and cut in half lengthwise	I medium green pepper, de-seeded and cut in half lengthwise
6 oz (170g) small button mushrooms	3 cups small button mushrooms
4 large tomatoes, each cut into 8 chunks	4 large tomatoes, each cut into 8 chunks
I bay leaf	I bay leaf
I level teaspoon oregano	I level teaspoon oregano
Sea salt and freshly ground black pepper	Sea salt and freshly ground black pepper
4 tablespoons finely grated Cheddar cheese	4 tablespoons finely grated Cheddar cheese

1 Wash beans and pick over for stones. Soak for 12 hours. Change the water 3 times. Rinse.

2 Bring to boil in fresh water. Boil for 10 minutes and then simmer for one hour or more until soft. Add the sea salt when the beans feel soft and will squash in your fingers. Cook for 10 minutes after this. Drain.

3 Set *slicing plate* in position. Stand onion upright in the feed tube, tightly packed. Slice. Scoop out. Leave slicing plate in position.

4 Heat oil in a pan. Sauté the onion and garlic until softish — approximately 5 minutes. Cover the pan.

5 Stand courgettes (zucchini) upright in the feed tube. If longer than the tube, cut in half. Pack tightly. Slice into circles. Press hard to get a reasonable thickness. Take out and sauté with the onion for 3 minutes.

6 Slice the green pepper, standing it upright in the feed tube. Press firmly down

with the pusher. Slice the mushrooms in the same way, arranging the caps to the outside of the feed tube.

7 Add these to the sautéing vegetables and continue to fry for 3 more minutes.

8 Now add the chopped tomatoes, bay leaf, oregano, sea salt and freshly ground black pepper. Cook for 1 minute.

9 Put drained beans in an shallow ovenproof baking dish. Pour over the vegetable mixture. Cover with foil and bake in a pre-heated oven at 325°F/160°C (Gas Mark 3) for 30 minutes. Take out, sprinkle with grated cheese and grill (broil) for a few minutes until lightly browned. Serve with boiled pot barley — see page 78 on how to cook this grain.

Spaghetti Bolognese
Serves 4 to 6

I have added a glass of red wine to this sauce, which adds a deliciously rich flavour to the mixture but is not essential. Add 1 tablespoon lemon juice if no wine is used. I use this sauce in my Lasagne, which follows this recipe. It is also delicious in the Stuffed Marrow recipe (see page 63).

Imperial (Metric)	American
2 oz (55g) almonds *or* hazelnuts	2 ounces almonds *or* hazelnuts
4 oz (115g) tvp mince, beef flavour	1 cup tvp mince, beef flavour
2 medium onions, peeled, roughly chopped	2 medium onions, peeled, roughly chopped
4 sticks celery, cut into 1 inch (2cm) pieces	4 stalks celery, cut into 1 inch pieces
3 tablespoons olive *or* sunflower oil	3 tablespoons olive *or* sunflower oil
2 cloves garlic, peeled and crushed	2 cloves garlic, peeled and crushed
1 heaped teaspoon basil	1 heaped teaspoon basil
1 bay leaf	1 bay leaf
1 green pepper, de-seeded and roughly chopped	1 green pepper, de-seeded and roughly chopped
4 oz (115g) mushrooms, washed and wiped	2 cups mushrooms, washed and wiped
12 oz (340g) tin tomatoes, chopped	12 ounces canned tomatoes, chopped
2 tablespoons tomato purée	2 tablespoons tomato paste
¼ pint (140ml) red wine	⅔ cup red wine
Freshly ground black pepper and sea salt to taste	Freshly ground black pepper and sea salt to taste

1 Set *fine shredding plate* in position. Pack the nuts into the feed tube. Grate.

2 Soak the tvp mince in the same volume of boiling water for 10 minutes.

3 Set *steel blades* in position. Chop finely the onion and celery. Scoop out. Keep blades in position.

4 Heat oil in a heavy-bottomed medium-sized saucepan. Sauté the onion, celery and garlic for 5 minutes. Keep lid on. Add the soya mince and sauté with the onion for 5 minutes more. Stir in the basil and bay leaf.

5 Place green pepper and mushrooms into the processor bowl. Chop finely.

6 Add these to the vegetable and mince and continue to fry for 3 more minutes only.

7 Stir in the grated nuts.

8 Add the tomatoes and the purée (paste) and red wine. Taste and add sea salt and freshly ground black pepper. Bring to boil, then turn down to simmer and let cook gently with the lid on for 25 to 30 minutes.

9 Serve on a bed of wholemeal spaghetti or buckwheat spaghetti (see note on buckwheat, page 76) which is very light in texture and a pleasant change. Sprinkle on grated Parmesan or tasty farmhouse Cheddar cheese. Serve with a bowl of crisp lettuce and cucumber dressed with a lemon and oil dressing.

Lasagne
Serves 6

For this recipe you can use wholemeal lasagne or wholewheat semolina lasagne verdi, which is a pasta made with semolina, wheatgrain and spinach. The wholemeal pasta has more nutritional value but I like to use the green lasagne as a change from the slightly heavier wholemeal varity.

Imperial (Metric)	American
8 oz (225g) lasagne	8 ounces lasagne
Sunflower oil	Sunflower oil
I teaspoon sea salt	I teaspoon sea salt
I recipe Bolognese Sauce (opposite)	I recipe Bolognese Sauce (opposite)
8 oz (225g) ricotta cheese *or* Quark	I cup ricotta cheese *or* Quark

For the cheese sauce:

Imperial (Metric)	American
2 oz (55g) 81 per cent wheat flour	½ cup 81 per cent wheat flour
½ teaspoon ground mace	½ teaspoon ground mace
½ teaspoon ground mustard	½ teaspoon ground mustard
1½ pints (850ml) milk	3¾ cups milk
3 oz (85g) finely grated Parmesan cheese *or* farmhouse Cheddar	¾ cup finely grated Parmesan cheese *or* farmhouse Cheddar
Sea salt and freshly ground black pepper	Sea salt and freshly ground black pepper
Oregano	Oregano

1 Rub the lasagne sheets with a little oil.

2 Bring a large pot of water to boil. Add the salt and drop the lasagne in sheet by sheet. Boil for 15 minutes or as directed on the packet.

3 Take sheets out with a fork and drape over the edge of a large colander.

4 Grease a large square or rectangular baking dish. Line the bottom with lasagne.

5 Spoon over half the Bolognese sauce.

6 Dot with half the soft cheese. Place another layer of lasagne on top.

7 Repeat with Bolognese and soft cheese, covering with a layer of pasta.

For the cheese sauce:

1 Set *steel blades* in position and put flour, mace, mustard and half the milk into the processor bowl. Blend until smooth. Gradually add the remaining milk with the motor still on.

2 Grease a heavy-based saucepan. Pour in the milk mixture. Bring to boil stirring constantly. Let simmer for 2 minutes only. Take off heat.

3 Stir in 2 oz (55g/½ cup) of the cheese. Taste and add sea salt and freshly ground black pepper to taste.

4 Pour over the lasagne. Sprinkle on the remaining cheese plus a little oregano. Bake in a pre-heated oven, 400°F/200°C (Gas Mark 6), for 20 minutes. Let stand for 10 minutes before serving. Serve with a fresh green salad.

Stuffed Marrow (Squash)
Serves 4

To stuff marrow (squash) I combine Bolognese sauce with a little cooked, short grain brown rice. So any left-overs from these can be frozen and used in this tasty dish.

Imperial (Metric)	American
1 medium marrow	1 long summer squash
½ recipe for Bolognese Sauce (see page 60)	½ recipe for Bolognese Sauce (see page 60)
6 oz (170g) cooked short grain Italian brown rice	1 cup cooked short grain Italian brown rice
2 oz (55g) grated cheese for topping	½ cup grated cheese for topping
Oregano	Oregano

For the cheese sauce:

Imperial (Metric)	American
Follow directions for the Lasagne Cheese Sauce (see page 61) but use 4 oz (115g) grated cheese	Follow directions for the Lasagne Cheese Sauce (see page 61) but use 1 cup grated cheese

1 Trim both ends of the marrow (squash). Slice into rings 1½ inches (4.5cm) thick. Remove the seeds, making a hole in each ring.

2 Steam the rings for 10 minutes.

3 Grease a large ovenproof baking dish. Place the rings in this.

4 Combine the Bolognese with the rice, and stuff the centre of each ring, mounding the top.

5 Pour over the cheese sauce.

6 Sprinkle on 2 oz (55g/½ cup) cheese and a little oregano.

7 Bake at 375°F/190°C (Gas Mark 5) for 40 minutes.

Hungarian Goulash
Serves 4

I use tvp chunks for this recipe but you can use one tin of red kidney beans, drained, or soak and cook 6 ounces (170g) dry weight kidney beans. Have a go with the chunks because the amount I use will cost you so little and give you as much protein as 12 ounces (340g) lean beef. The sauce is so piquant that it is absorbed by the chunks and the dish is quite delicious.

Imperial (Metric)	American
4 oz (115g) tvp beef flavoured soya chunks	4 ounces tvp beef flavoured soy chunks
2 medium onions, peeled and cut in quarters lengthwise	2 medium onions, peeled and cut in quarters lengthwise
I large green pepper, de-seeded	I large green pepper, de-seeded
3 tablespoons sunflower *or* olive oil	3 tablespoons sunflower *or* olive oil
I large clove garlic, crushed	I large clove garlic, crushed
I bay leaf	I bay leaf
I vegetable stock cube	I vegetable stock cube
Freshly ground black pepper	Freshly ground black pepper
2 tablespoons paprika	2 tablespoons paprika
I level tablespoon wholemeal flour	I level tablespoon wholewheat flour
I lb 12 oz (795g) tinned tomatoes, chopped	I pound 12 ounces canned tomatoes, chopped
I tablespoon tomato purée	I tablespoon tomato paste
4 tablespoons thick natural yogurt	4 tablespoons thick plain yogurt
2 tablespoons double cream	2 tablespoons heavy cream
Finely chopped parsley to garnish	Finely chopped parsley to garnish

1 Soak the soya chunks for at least 4 hours in enough boiling water to cover them by 1 inch (2.5cm) or follow packet instructions for quick hydration. Drain.

2 Set *slicing plate* in position. Pack onion pieces in feed tube, standing upright. Slice. Scoop out.

3 Place cut peppers in the feed tube in an upright position. Slice.

4 Heat oil in a pan. Sauté the onion and garlic for 7 minutes with lid on.

5 Add the green pepper and continue to fry for 3 minutes.

6 Stir in the bay leaf, crumbled stock cube, freshly ground black pepper, the paprika and the drained soya chunks.

7 Fry all on gentle heat for 3 minutes.

8 Stir in the flour and cook, stirring constantly, for 1 minute.

9 Add the tomatoes and tomato purée (paste). Stir together. Bring to boil. Turn down to simmer and cover. Let simmer for 1 hour — or bake in the oven in a tight-lidded casserole dish, 375°F/190°C (Gas Mark 5), for 1½ hours. Whisk together the yogurt and cream and stir in before serving. Garnish with parsley.

Wholegrains, Nuts and Seeds and Vegetable Dishes

Wholegrains

Wholegrains, besides being a valuable source of protein, vitamins and minerals, also contain fibre which our body needs if it is to function properly.

During the process of refining, when the outer layers are removed the grains are stripped of their nutrients and fibre and what is left is virtually pure carbohydrate. The whole miraculous natural balance which is packed into one tiny grain is destroyed. Through eating the whole grain we absorb the goodness and the fibre helps get rid of unwanted body waste.

Nuts and seeds

Although nuts and seeds have a high fat content, they are rich in linoleic acid, particularly the seeds, which helps control the level of cholesterol in the body. They are also a high-protein food and rich in minerals and vitamins.

Try to avoid salted nuts as these are often treated with preservatives, colourings and other inhibiting chemicals which can cause problems to the digestive system.

As previously mentioned, wholegrains, nuts and seeds will make complete protein meals when used in the right combination; see page 8 for notes on protein foods. To balance a meal based on wholegrains, include approximately 50 per cent grains with 25 per cent pulses, nuts and seeds or dairy produce, or a combination of all three and 25 per cent fresh vegetables.

Brown rice

Brown rice has the fibre, protein, vitamins and minerals all intact. Eating white rice is virtually eating pure carbohydrate — starch. It is important to learn to cook brown rice well and, as there are several varieties, it is not always easy to do this. For plain Italian short or long grain rice, wash the rice well, add just under double its volume in cold water plus a little sea salt. Bring to the boil, turn down to simmer and cook with a tight lid for 35 to 40 minutes. For Surinam or Australian long thin brown rice the cooking time is 25 minutes.

Toasted Almond Rice with Lemon or Spiced Tomato Sauce

You can use toasted cashews or pistachio nuts for this recipe and vary the vegetables according to what is in season.

Imperial (Metric)	American
4 oz (115g) almonds (skins on)	I cup almonds (skins on)
12 oz (340g) short grain Italian brown rice	I½ cups short grain Italian brown rice
I teaspoon sea salt	I teaspoon sea salt
I bay leaf	I bay leaf
I cinnamon stick	I cinnamon stick
I medium onion, peeled	I medium onion, peeled
I clove garlic, crushed	I clove garlic, crushed
2 medium carrots, scraped	2 medium carrots, scraped
4 tablespoons sunflower oil	4 tablespoons sunflower oil
4 oz (115g) small button mushrooms, whole or halved	4 ounces small button mushrooms, whole or halved
6 oz (170g) French beans, cooked and cut into I inch (2.5cm) pieces	6 ounces snap beans, cooked and cut into I inch pieces

For the lemon sauce:

Imperial (Metric)	American
2 tablespoons fresh chopped parsley	2 tablespoons fresh chopped parsley
Finely grated rind of I lemon	Finely grated rind of I lemon
Juice of I lemon	Juice of I lemon
½ teaspoon allspice *or* ground nutmeg	½ teaspoon allspice *or* ground nutmeg
½ teaspoon freshly ground black pepper	½ teaspoon freshly ground black pepper
I tablespoon shoyu (naturally fermented soya sauce)	I tablespoon naturally fermented soy sauce

1 Place almonds on a baking tray and bake in the oven at 375°F/190°C (Gas Mark 5) for 20 minutes, or until the centres are golden-brown.

2 Measure out rice in cupfuls. Wash well by placing in a sieve and letting cold water run through the grains for 1 minute. Drain and place in a heavy based saucepan.

3 Add double the volume of rice in cold water, plus the sea salt, bay leaf and cinnamon stick. Bring to boil then turn down to simmer. Cover with a tight lid

and let cook for 35 minutes. Do not stir. The water should all be absorbed by the end of cooking time. If not, take out the bay leaf and cinnamon stick and drain through a colander. Spread rice on a large flat plate or turn and let excess moisture dry off.

4 Set *slicing plate* in position. Cut onion lengthwise and pack into feed tube in an upright position. Slice. Cut carrots in half widthwise and pack into the feed tube in an upright position. Slice into circles.

5 Place 2 tablespoons oil in a large heavy-based saucepan. Sauté the carrots, onion and garlic for 7 minutes. Add the mushrooms and the chopped beans. Stir and cook for 1 minute on moderate heat. Add the remaining oil, stir in the rice and toss with the vegetables for 1 minute.

6 Add three-quarters of the toasted almonds. Mix most of the parsley, lemon rind and juice, allspice, black pepper and shoyu (soy sauce) together. Trickle this over the rice. Let the flavours merge in the hot pan for 10 minutes. Put into a serving dish and garnish with the remaining almonds and a little fresh chopped parsley. Lovely hot or cold.

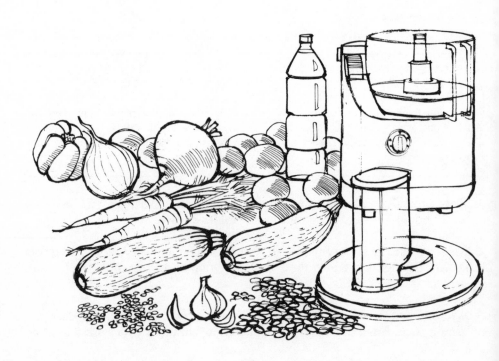

Variation:

Toasted Almond Rice with Spiced Tomato Sauce

All you do is exclude the lemon sauce and substitute with the following sauce mixture.

Imperial (Metric)	American
14 oz (395g) tin tomatoes	14 ounce can tomatoes
1 tablespoon tomato purée	1 tablespoon tomato paste
1 large clove garlic, crushed	1 large clove garlic, crushed
1 green eating apple, peeled and roughly chopped	1 green eating apple, peeled and roughly chopped
½ green and ½ red pepper, roughly chopped	½ green and ½ red pepper, roughly chopped
2 tablespoons grated celeriac *or* 1 teaspoon celery seeds, crushed	2 tablespoons grated celeriac *or* 1 teaspoon celery seeds, crushed
1 teaspoon basil	1 teaspoon basil
½ teaspoon tarragon	½ teaspoon tarragon
1 tablespoon lemon juice	1 tablespoon lemon juice
1 tablespoon shoyu (naturally fermented soya sauce)	1 tablespoon naturally fermented soy sauce
1 teaspoon Tabasco sauce *or* 1 level teaspoon cayenne pepper	1 teaspoon Tabasco sauce *or* 1 level teaspoon cayenne pepper

1 Set *steel blades* in position. Put all the ingredients into the processor bowl. Blend until smooth.

2 Cook this purée on low heat until some of the liquid evaporates and the sauce is thick, about 20 minutes. Pour over the rice and almond mixture just before serving. Garnish with a few toasted almonds and a little chopped parsley.

Note: The spiced tomato sauce is delicious with rissoles or as a barbecue dip.

Bulgur Wheat Arabian Style
Serves 4

Traditionally couscous, which is a grain produced from semolina, is used for this recipe, but I prefer the flavour of bulgur which is a cracked wholewheat product and nutritionally superior. In North Africa a couscousier is used to cook this dish, but I have used a muslin-lined steamer or snug fitting muslin-lined colander placed on top of a deep saucepan with success.

Imperial (Metric)	American
6 oz (170g) chick peas, dry weight	I cup dry garbanzo beans

For the Bulgur:

Imperial (Metric)	American
12 oz (340g) bulgur wheat	2 cups bulgur wheat
¾ pint (425ml) cold water and a little sea salt	2 cups cold water and a little sea salt
2 tablespoons olive oil	2 tablespoons olive oil

For the vegetable sauce:

Imperial (Metric)	American
8 oz (225g) onion (weight when peeled), cut in half	8 ounces onion (weight when peeled), cut in half
2 large carrots, scraped	2 large carrots, scraped
8 oz (225g) potatoes, scrubbed	8 ounces potatoes, scrubbed
I kohlrabi or turnip, peeled	I kohlrabi or turnip, peeled
6 oz (170g) celeriac	6 ounces celeriac
3 tablespoons olive or sesame seed oil	3 tablespoons olive or sesame seed oil
2 large cloves garlic, peeled and crushed	2 large cloves garlic, peeled and crushed
I tablespoon shoyu (naturally fermented soya sauce)	I tablespoon naturally fermented soy sauce
Freshly ground black pepper	Freshly ground black pepper
2 medium courgettes	2 medium zucchini
I large green pepper, de-seeded	I large green pepper, de-seeded
I teaspoon coriander seeds, crushed	I teaspoon coriander seeds, crushed
I teaspoon cumin seeds, crushed	I teaspoon cumin seeds, crushed
I teaspoon turmeric	I teaspoon turmeric
14 oz (395g) tin tomatoes	14 ounce can tomatoes
	I tablespoon tomato paste

I tablespoon tomato purée	⅔ cup raisins
4 oz (115g) raisins	I teaspoon Tabasco sauce *or* I level
I teaspoon Tabasco sauce *or* I level	teaspoon cayenne pepper
teaspoon cayenne pepper	I tablespoon lemon juice
I tablespoon lemon juice	2 cups water
¾ (425ml) water	

---

1 Wash the chick peas (garbanzo beans) and pick over for stones. Soak overnight. Rinse and cook in fresh water for 1 to 1¼ hours until soft. Add 1 teaspoon sea salt 10 minutes before the end of cooking time.

2 Put the bulgur in a bowl. Pour over the cold water. Drain and rub in the olive oil with your fingertips. Rub again several times during the next 10 minutes. This keeps the grains separate.

3 Put *slicing plate* in position. Slice onion. Cut carrots lenthwise, then in half widthwise. Pack in feed tube and slice. Cut potatoes and kohlrabi in quarters lengthwise. Pack 2 quarters at a time into the feed tube and slice. Cut celeriac into thickish fingers. Stand upright in feed tube and slice. Keep slicing plate in position.

4 Heat oil in a large heavy-based saucepan. Sauté the onion, garlic, carrots, potatoes, kohlrabi and celeriac for 10 minutes. Toss to cook all evenly. Taste and add the shoyu (soy sauce) and black pepper. Add more shoyu (soy sauce) if you wish.

5 Cut courgettes (zucchini) in half lengthwise, pack standing upright in the feed tube and slice. Cut pepper in quarters and pack standing upright in the feed tube. Slice.

6 Add these to the other vegetables and cook gently for 3 minutes.

7 Stir in the drained chick peas (garbanzo beans), coriander, cumin and turmeric. Stir, tossing the vegetables in the spices for 1 minute.

8 Chop the tinned tomatoes and stir these into the vegetables with the tomato purée (paste), raisins, Tabasco, lemon juice and water. Bring to boil then turn down to simmer.

9 Place soaked bulgur in a lined colander or steamer. Place over simmering vegetables. Place lid or foil on top. Let simmer for 25 to 30 minutes.

To assemble the meal:

10 Pour bulgur into a large serving dish. Fork in a little olive oil to keep the grains separate. The sauce goes in the centre of the bulgur. Decorate with sprigs of watercress or coriander leaves (cilantro). Serve with yogurt and chopped cucumber salad.

Baked Bulgur Wheat and Cheese Pilaf
Serves 4

In this recipe I have used tamari sunflower seeds. Tamari is a thicker and more expensive than shoyu (naturally fermented from soya sauce) and is fermented soya beans, whereas shoyu is produced from fermented soya beans and wheat. You can toast your own seeds with shoyu. They are delicious with drinks and a healthy alternative to crisps. At the end of the recipe I have given instructions on toasting the seeds.

Imperial (Metric)	American
1½ pints (850ml) water	3¾ cups water
I vegetable stock cube	I vegetable stock cube
12 oz (340g) bulgur wheat	2 cups bulgur wheat
I large carrot, scraped	I large carrot, scraped
I medium onion, peeled and cut in half	I medium onion, peeled and cut in half
2 tablespoons olive oil or sunflower oil	2 tablespoons olive oil or sunflower oil
I large clove garlic, peeled and crushed	I large clove garlic, peeled and crushed
4 oz (100g) button mushrooms	2 cups button mushrooms
I tablespoon lemon juice	I tablespoon lemon juice
3 tablespoons fresh chopped parsley	3 tablespoons fresh chopped parsley
I teaspoon oregano	I teaspoon oregano
3 oz (85g) tamari sunflower seeds	¾ cup tamari sunflower seeds
4 oz (115g) grated farmhouse Cheddar cheese.	I cup grated farmhouse Cheddar cheese

1 Bring water to boil. Add stock cube. Put bulgur in a mixing bowl. Pour over the stock water. Cover and let stand to swell for 30 minutes.

2 Cut carrot into 1 inch (2.5cm) long thin sticks.

3 Set *slicing plate* in position. Slice onion. Scoop out. Leave plate in position.

4 Heat oil in a pan. Sauté carrot, onion and garlic for 7 minutes.

5 Slice mushrooms by packing them into the feed tube, caps to the outside.

6 Add these to the sautéd vegetables. Continue to fry for 3 more minutes.

7 Add lemon juice, parsley, oregano and sunflower seeds and cook on medium heat for 1 minute, tossing lightly together.

8 Fork into the bulgur mixture.

9 Transfer to an overproof baking dish or casserole base. Sprinkle on the cheese and bake for 10 minutes uncovered. If you want a golden brown top, just place under the grill for a few minutes. I prefer the cheese melted rather than crisp.

Note: To make your own Shoyu or Tamari Sunflower Seeds, simply toast the seeds in the oven at 325°F/160°C (Gas Mark 3) for 15 minutes. Sprinkle with a little soya sauce and bake for a further 5 minutes.

Baked Millet Pilaf
Serves 4-5

Millet is widely used in the African continent, India and Asia. It is well balanced in essential amino acids, rich in iron and has a lovely nutty flavour. It is also gluten-free for those on a gluten-free diet and makes delicious croquettes and cake-like bread.

Imperial (Metric)	American
3 tablespoons sunflower oil	3 tablespoons sunflower oil
8 oz (225g) wholegrain millet	1 cup wholegrain millet
1 large onion, peeled	1 large onion, peeled
2 medium carrots, scraped	2 medium carrots, scraped
2 sticks celery, washed	2 stalks celery, washed
1 small red pepper	1 small red pepper
4 oz (115g) small button mushrooms	2 cups small button mushrooms
1 clove garlic, crushed	1 clove garlic, crushed
2 tablespoons fresh chopped parsley	2 tablespoons fresh chopped parsley
1 teaspoon dried marjoram *or*	1 teaspoon dried marjoram *or*
1 dessertspoon fresh chopped leaves	2 teaspoons fresh chopped leaves
½ teaspoon cayenne pepper (optional)	½ teaspoon cayenne pepper (optional)
½ teaspoon freshly ground black pepper	½ teaspoon freshly ground black pepper
1 teaspoon herb salt *or* 1 vegetable stock	1 teaspoon herb salt *or* 1 vegetable stock
cube	cube
1½ pints (850ml) hot water	3¾ cups hot water
1 tablespoon lemon juice	1 tablespoon lemon juice
4 oz (115g) crumbled Lancashire cheese	1 cup crumbled Lancashire cheese
2 medium tomatoes, sliced in thin rings	2 medium tomatoes, sliced in thin rings
Marjoram, for topping	Marjoram, for topping

1 Heat 1 tablespoon oil in a heavy-bottomed saucepan. Toast the millet on moderate heat for approximately 5 minutes. Stir all the time with a wooden spoon. Do not burn. Place this in a casserole dish.

2 Set *slicing plate* in position. Cut onion lengthwise. Pack standing upright into the feed tube. Slice. Cut carrots in half lengthwise and pack in feed tube, standing upright. Slice and scoop out.

3 Cut celery into lengths as long as the feed tube. Pack in, standing upright. Slice. Cut pepper in quarters, stand upright in the feed tube and slice. Wash and wipe mushrooms, pack in feed tube with caps to the outside and slice.

4 Heat the 2 tablespoons oil in a pan. Sauté the onion, carrot and garlic for 5 minutes. Add the celery, red pepper and mushrooms and continue to sauté for 3 more minutes.

5 Stir in parsley, marjoram, cayenne and black pepper.

6 Fork the vegetables into the toasted millet.

7 Stir the herb salt or stock cube into the hot water and add the lemon juice. Pour this over the millet mixture. Stir well in.

8 Sprinkle on the crumbled cheese. Arrange the tomato slices on top and dress with a little more marjoram. (Don't worry if the cheese and tomato look like sinking. They will float to the top during baking.)

9 Place a piece of foil over the top then press the lid firmly on. Make it as airtight as possible.

10 Bake in a pre-heated at oven 350°F/180°C (Gas Mark 4) for 1 hour.

Note: Delicious with lightly cooked spinach or spring greens.

Toasted Buckwheat Savoury
Serves 4

Buckwheat has a very distinctive flavour and is quite delicious with a piquant vegetable sauce. It contains rutic acid which is known to have a good effect on the circulatory system, is rich in iron and the B vitamins. It is best to buy already toasted buckwheat which only takes 20 minutes to cook.

Imperial (Metric)	American
1 tablespoon olive oil	1 tablespoon olive oil
8 oz (225g) toasted buckwheat	1⅓ cups toasted buckwheat
1½ pints (850ml) boiling water	4 cups boiling water
1 very level teaspoon sea salt	1 very level teaspoon sea salt
2 medium onions, peeled	2 medium onions, peeled
1 clove garlic, crushed	1 clove garlic, crushed
2 tablespoons olive oil	2 tablespoons olive oil
2 medium courgettes	2 medium zucchini
1 green pepper	1 green pepper
8 oz (225g) fresh ripe tomatoes	8 ounces fresh ripe tomatoes
2 tablespoons lemon juice	2 tablespoons lemon juice
1 level teaspoon coriander	1 level teaspoon coriander
1 level teaspoon paprika	1 level teaspoon paprika
½ cinnamon stick	½ cinnamon stick
1 bay leaf	1 bay leaf
1 teaspoon fresh chopped mint leaves	1 teaspoon fresh chopped mint leaves

1 In a heavy-based saucepan heat the oil and stir the buckwheat over gentle heat for 2 minutes. Pour on the boiling water. Add the salt and simmer on low heat with lid on for 20 minutes.

2 Set *slicing plate* in position. Cut onions in half and slice. Scoop out and leave plate in position.

3 Heat 2 tablespoons olive oil in a pan, sauté the onion and garlic for 5 minutes with lid on.

4 Wash courgettes (zucchini), and trim and cut in half widthwise. Pack upright into the feed tube and slice. Scoop out. Keep slicing plate in position.

5 Add these to the onion and garlic and continue to fry for 3 minutes more.

6 Wash and de-seed the pepper. Cut lengthwise and pack into the feed tube in an upright position. Slice and scoop out.

7 Sauté these with the other vegetables for 3 minutes.

8 Skin the tomatoes by cutting a circle around the stalk end and immersing in boiling water for 5 minutes. Then peel.

9 Set *steel blades* in position. Blend tomatoes, lemon juice, coriander and paprika until smooth.

10 Pour this over the sautéd vegetables. Add the cinnamon stick, the bay leaf and the mint. Stir well. Simmer with lid on for 15 minutes. Stir occasionally.

11 Serve the buckwheat and the sauce in separate bowls. The buckwheat is very soft when cooked and will become soggy if mixed with the sauce too soon before eating.

Pot Barley Bake
Serves 4

Barley is a much neglected grain when it comes to main meals. Most of us use it in stews but it is quite delicious as an alternative to rice. Pot barley is the whole grain whereas pearl barley is refined and lacks most of the germ and fibre. It is an easily digested food, so it is helpful for those who have digestive problems.

Imperial (Metric)	American
12 oz (340g) pot barley	1½ cups pot barley
1½ pints (850ml) water for soaking	3¾ cups water for soaking
1 level teaspoon sea salt	1 level teaspoon sea salt
2 medium onions, peeled	2 medium onions, peeled
3 tablespoons sunflower oil	3 tablespoons sunflower oil
1 clove garlic, crushed	1 clove garlic, crushed
3 oz (85g) tvp mince	¾ cup tvp mince
4 sticks celery	4 stalks celery
4 oz (115g) mushrooms	4 ounces mushrooms
1 level teaspoon basil	1 level teaspoon basil
2 tablespoons fresh chopped parsley	2 tablespoons fresh chopped parsley
Freshly ground black pepper	Freshly ground black pepper
6 medium tomatoes	6 medium tomatoes
1 tablespoon tomato purée	1 tablespoon tomato paste
1 tablespoon shoyu	1 tablespoon naturally fermented soy sauce

For the topping:

Imperial (Metric)	American
2 eggs	2 eggs
8 fl oz (225ml) natural yogurt and milk, mixed	1 cupful plain yogurt and milk, mixed
Sea salt and freshly ground black pepper	Sea salt and freshly ground black pepper
2 oz (55g) grated farmhouse Cheddar cheese	2 ounces grated farmhouse Cheddar cheese

1 Wash barley and soak for 6 hours or overnight.

2 Bring to boil in soaking water and sea salt. Let simmer with the lid on for 20 to 25 minutes. Drain and save 7 fl oz (200ml/¾ cup) of the cooking water, if any is left.

3 Set *slicing plate* in position. Cut onions in half lengthwise and pack each half into the feed tube. Slice.

4 Heat oil in heavy-based saucepan. Sauté the onion and garlic for 10 minutes with the lid on.

5 Soak the tvp mince in the retained barley water or just hot water for 10 minutes, until it has swollen and absorbed the liquid.

6 Sauté this with the onion for 5 minutes, stirring and coating the mince with the onion and garlic.

7 Set *steel blades* in position. Cut celery in smallish chunks, wash and wipe the mushroms. Place the celery and the whole mushrooms into the processor bowl and chop finely. Scoop out.

8 Add this to the onions and mince. Stir in the parsley, basil and freshly ground black pepper and fry in gentle heat for 3 minutes.

9 Skin tomatoes by cutting a circle round the stalk end and immerse in boiling water for 5 minutes, then peel. With steel blades still in position blend tomatoes with the tomatoe purée (paste) and shoyu (soy sauce) until smooth.

10 Pour this into the mince and vegetable mixture. Cook gently for a few minutes only.

11 Pour this into a greased baking dish. Spoon the barley over the top.

For the topping:

1 Set *steel blades* in position, blend eggs, yogurt, milk, sea salt and black pepper for a few seconds.

2 Pour this over the barley and sprinkle on the cheese.

3 Bake in pre-heated oven, 375°F/190°C (Gas Mark 5), for 25 minutes. If liked, place under the grill (broiler) if top is not golden brown enough. Absolutely delicious served with lightly cooked spring greens or broccoli tops.

Vegetable Curry
Serves 4/5

To begin this recipe I will give you my favourite medley of spices that will turn any assortment of vegetables into an authentic tasting curry.

Basic curry powder mixture:

Imperial (Metric)	American
2 level tablespoons turmeric	2 level tablespoons turmeric
2 level tablespoons cumin	2 level tablespoons cumin
2 level tablespoons coriander	2 level tablespoons coriander
I dessertspoon chilli powder	2 teaspoons chili powder
16 cardamoms, podded and crushed	16 cardamoms, podded and crushed
I level teaspoon clove powder	I level teaspoon clove powder
I very level tablespoon black mustard seeds, crushed	I very level tablespoon black mustard seeds, crushed

Just mix all well together and place in an airtight jar. Other ingredients, such as fresh grated ginger, cinnamon sticks, curry leaves or methi (fenugreek leaves) and tamarind can also be added, but the basic mix is always useful to have ready. Tamarind looks like pressed dates. It has hard seeds and a tangy delicious taste. If not available you can substitute with lemon juice.

For the curry:

Imperial (Metric)	American
2 medium onions, peeled	2 medium onions, peeled
2 cloves garlic, crushed	2 cloves garlic, crushed
3 medium potatoes, scrubbed and diced into I inch (2.5cm) cubes	3 medium potatoes, scrubbed and diced into I-inch cubes
3 tablespoons sunflower oil	3 tablespoons sunflower oil
½ medium cauliflower, cut into florets	½ medium cauliflower, cut into florets
3 sticks celery, washed	3 stalks celery, washed
2 medium courgettes	2 medium zucchini
I green pepper, de-seeded	I green pepper, de-seeded
I small cooking apple, thinly peeled and cored	I small cooking apple, thinly peeled and cored
I slightly rounded tablespoon curry powder mixture (above)	I slightly rounded tablespoon curry powder mixture (above)
I cinnamon stick	I cinnamon stick

I dessertspoon methi *or* curry leaves	2 teaspoons methi *or* curry leaves
I rounded dessertspoon wholemeal flour	2 rounded teaspoons wholewheat flour
2 oz (55g) piece of tamarind soaked in ¼ pint (140ml) hot water, *or*	2 ounces tamarind soaked in ⅔ cup hot water, *or*
juice of I lemon	juice of I lemon
½ teaspoon finely grated fresh ginger	½ teaspoon finely grated fresh ginger
6 oz (170g) French beans *or* okra, trimmed	6 ounces French beans *or* okra, trimmed
4 medium tomatoes, skinned (not tinned) and chopped	4 medium tomatoes, skinned (not canned) and chopped
I tablespoon tomato purée	I tablespoon tomato paste
7 fl oz (200ml) hot water	¾ cup hot water
Sea salt *or* stock cube	Sea salt *or* stock cube

---

1 Set *slicing plate* in position. Cut onions in half lengthwise. Pack each half into feed tube and slice. Scoop out. Replace the slicing plate.

2 Heat oil in a large heavy-based saucepan. Sauté onion, garlic and potato cubes for 10 minutes on moderate heat with lid on.

3 Stir in cauliflower florets and continue to sauté for 5 minutes.

4 Cut celery into sticks just under the length of feed tube. Cut courgettes (zucchini) in half widthwise. Cut green pepper in quarters lengthwise. Slice all in turn, packing them in the feed tube in an upright position. Press the pusher firmly to achieve thicker slices. Slice apple in the same way.

5 Stir these into the vegetables and continue to fry for 3 more minutes.

6 Add curry powder, cinnamon stick, methi *or* curry leaves and wholemeal (wholewheat) flour and toss the vegetables on low heat for 2 minutes only.

7 Strain the soaking tamarind in a sieve, pressing as much pulp through as possible. You will end up with a smooth runny brown liquid. To this add the ginger.

8 Stir this into the vegetables. Add green beans or okra whole. Stir in, cover pot and take off heat.

9 Set *steel blades* in position. Blend together the tomatoes, tomato purée (paste) and water until smooth. Stir this into the sautéd vegetables. Re-heat slowly, taste and add sea salt or a crumbled vegetable stock cube. Let simmer very gently with a lid on for 20 to 25 minutes only. The vegetables should still be reasonably firm.

Saffron Rice
Serves 4

I use Surinam or Australian long, thin brown rice with curry. It only takes 25 minutes to cook and is lighter in texture than the Italian variety.

Imperial (Metric)	American
2 cups Surinam brown rice	2½ cups Surinam brown rice
4 cups water	5 cups water
I teaspoon sea salt	I teaspoon sea salt
I dessertspoon sunflower *or* sesame seed oil	2 teaspoons sunflower *or* sesame seed oil
½ teaspoon powdered saffron *or* turmeric	½ teaspoon powdered saffron *or* turmeric

1 Measure out the rice before washing. Place in a sieve and let cold water run through the grains for 1 minute.

2 Place in a heavy-based, medium-sized saucepan. Add the water, sea salt, oil and saffron or turmeric.

3 Bring to boil, turn down to simmer. Cover with a tightly fitting lid (if not tight fitting, place a sheet of baking foil over the top then put the lid on firmly). Let simmer for 25 minutes. Take off heat. Let stand covered for 5 minutes. It is now ready to serve.

Note: Serve the curry and rice with a dhal. I suggest the Lentil and Mushroom Pâté on page 28, since it is a type of dhal mixture. Just add 1 teacupful of water to the ingredients and you will have the soft consistency of dhal. I also serve a curry with a bowl of thick natural yogurt to which I have added chopped cucumber and a little clear honey.

I will now give you three other accompaniments that are a real treat with a curry meal: Chapatis, Puris and Samosas. Choose Chapatis *or* Puris as a side dish and the Samosas are wonderful to give to your guests as an appetizer. Try to get wholemeal chapati flour as this is lighter than normal wholemeal flour.

Chapati and Puri Unyeasted Dough

Makes approximately 10 to 12 Chapatis or 24 Puris.

For the dough:

Imperial (Metric)	American
12 oz (340g) wholemeal chapati flour	3 cups wholemeal chapati flour
I very level teaspoon sea salt	I very level teaspoon sea salt
8 fl oz (225ml) water	I cup water
3 tablespoons (45ml) cold-pressed sunflower or virgin olive oil	3 tablespoons cold-pressed sunflower or virgin olive oil

1 Set *steel blades* in position and put flour and sea salt into the bowl.

2 Mix water and oil together and with motor running, pour the liquid into the feed tube. Continue to process until you have a smooth, shiny dough.

3 Put dough into an oiled plastic bag and leave to rest for 1 to 2 hours.

To make chapatis:

1 Divide the dough into 10 to 12 balls, depending on what size you want your chapatis to be.

2 Take each ball in turn just before cooking and flatten between the palms of your hands, then flip it from palm to palm a few times.

3 Roll out on a floured surface to approximately 7 inches (18cm) in diameter.

4 Heat a non-stick frying pan or griddle and, when hot, put in the chapati, pressing it gently with the back of a large spoon to encourage it to bubble in places.

5 When underside is turning brown, lightly flip it over and cook the other side.

6 Keep each one warm in oven while you are cooking. These can be served instead of rice with your curry or as an extra. You can also add crushed black peppercorns or coriander seeds for extra flavour.

To make the puris:

These are fried, so you will need corn, peanut or soya oil.

1 Using the same dough as for chapatis, pinch off walnut-sized pieces and roll into balls.

2 Flatten each on an oiled surface with an oiled rolling pin to about 3 inches (8cm) in diameter.

3 Heat oil in a deep frying pan and drop in one at a time. As soon as the puri surfaces (which is almost immediately) press it gently with the back of a large spoon. It will puff up like a balloon or puff up in parts.

4 When lightly golden turn over and fry other side for a few seconds only. Delicious eaten at once, but they will keep in a warm oven for a short time.

Samosas (Curried Vegetable Pasties)
Makes approx. 8-10

For the dough:

Imperial (Metric)	American
6 oz (170g) wholemeal chapati flour	1½ cups wholewheat chapati flour
½ teaspoon sea salt	½ teaspoon sea salt
3 tablespoons corn or sunflower oil	3 tablespoons corn or sunflower oil
4 fl oz (120ml) natural yogurt	½ cup plain yogurt
Sunflower, corn or soya oil for deep frying	Sunflower, corn or soya oil for deep frying

1 Set *steel blades* in position. Put flour, sea salt, oil and yogurt into the bowl. Process until a soft dough is formed.

2 Shape into a ball and put in a polythene bag. Leave to stand for 30 minutes or as long as it takes you to prepare and cool the filling (see below).

3 When filling is cool, roll out the dough thinly and cut into 2½ inch (6cm) squares.

4 Place 2 generous teaspoons of the filling on one half of the square. Brush edges with milk or water and fold over each square corner to corner to form a triangle.

5 Heat oil and fry just a few at a time until golden brown. Drain on absorbent kitchen paper and serve hot.

For the filling:

You can use any mixture for the filling. The Spicy Lentil and Mushroom Pâté on page 28 is very suitable. Any left-over curry mixture will do as long as it is not too wet. But I like this very simple, quick-to-prepare stuffing, the ingredients of which are usually in the store cupboard.

Imperial (Metric)	American
1 medium onion	1 medium onion
1 tablespoon corn *or* sunflower oil	1 tablespoon corn *or* sunflower oil
1 clove garlic, crushed	1 clove garlic, crushed
1 rounded teaspoon fresh ginger, grated	1 rounded teaspoon fresh ginger, grated
1 rounded teaspoon garam masala	1 rounded teaspoon garam masala
1 very level teaspoon cayenne *or* chilli powder	1 very level teaspoon cayenne *or* chili powder
1 teaspoon methi (fenugreek leaf) (optional)	1 teaspoon methi (fenugreek leaf) (optional)
½ lb (225g) potatoes, steamed with skins on	½ pound potatoes, steamed with skins on
4 oz (115g) frozen peas, cooked for 3 minutes only	1 cup frozen peas, cooked for 3 minutes only
A little sea salt	A little sea salt

1 Set *slicing plate* in position. Peel and cut onion lengthwise. Put each half into feed tube in an upright position. Insert pusher and slice.

2 Heat oil in a pan and sauté the onion and garlic until soft, about 5 minutes. Add the ginger, garam masala, cayenne or chilli, and methi and cook on low heat for 2 minutes.

3 Leaving skins on potatoes, chop roughly. Set *steel blades* in position and mash potato.

4 Add potato and peas to the onion and spice mixture. Stir well in and let cook for 2 minutes only. Taste and add a little sea salt if you wish. There should be no moisture left. Cool and proceed as directed in the Samosa dough recipe above.

Pancakes (Crêpes), and Other Batters

Pancake (crêpe) batter makes a lovely base for many savoury and sweet fillings. The basic mixture which I will give can have vegetables like spinach, broccoli and parsley blended in to give extra flavour and goodness. You can also add finely chopped onion and peppers, sweetcorn and cheese and make the mixture into small fritters which are a simple meal in themselves. I use 100 per cent wholemeal (wholewheat) flour for pancakes (crêpes) I am going to stuff, but for a fritter batter I mix soya flour with wholemeal to add more protein (soya flour is approximately 38 per cent protein). Another delicious batter which I make for Tempura (deep fried battered vegetables, page 92) is a mixture of gram (chick pea /garbanzo flour), brown rice flour, and soya flour. A crêpe or pancake pan is a great help in making perfect pancakes. It is a small heavy pan with gently sloping edges. The base is 7 inches (18cm) in diameter.

Basic Pancake (Crêpe) Batter
Makes 12

Imperial (Metric)	American
4 oz (115g) wholemeal flour	4 ounces wholewheat flour
2 large eggs	2 large eggs
½ pint (285ml) milk	1⅓ cups milk
½ teaspoon sea salt	½ teaspoon sea salt
2 tablespoons olive oil *or* sunflower oil	2 tablespoons olive oil *or* sunflower oil
Extra oil for frying	Extra oil for frying

1 Set *steel blades* in position. Blend flour, eggs, half the milk, and sea salt until smooth.

2 With motor still on, gradually add the remaining milk, followed by the oil.

3 Pour into a mixing bowl and let stand for 2 hours. The starchy cells will swell, the batter will thicken slightly and your pancakes (crêpes) will be much lighter. Beat vigorously.

4 Have a small bowl of oil, plus a piece of kitchen paper screwed into a ball, at the ready. Dip the paper into the oil and wipe it over the base of the pan, leaving a thin coat of oil on the surface. Heat well.

5 Drop 2 tablespoons of the batter into the pan. Tilt it so that the batter covers the base. It will cook in about half a minute (watch the heat — turn it up and down to avoid burning).

6 Toss it over with a palette knife and cook the other side for just under half a minute. The first one might stick but as you regulate your heat and the pan stays hot this will not happen. These can be stacked one on top of the other until you are ready to fill them. They can also be frozen successfully. Defrost completely and peel off each one carefully.

Parsley Pancakes (Crêpes) with Leeks, Mushrooms and White Wine
Serves 4

The white wine is a luxury and not essential. Add it if you are making this for a dinner party. You will probably have to buy 2 pounds (900g) of leeks to get 1 pound (450g) when trimmed.

Imperial (Metric)	American
1 recipe for Basic Pancake Batter (opposite)	1 recipe for Basic Crêpe Batter (opposite)
2 oz (55g) fresh parsley sprigs (stems included)	2 ounces fresh parsley sprigs (stems included)
1 lb (455g) leeks, when trimmed	1 pound of leeks, when trimmed
3 tablespoons sunflower oil	3 tablespoons sunflower oil
8 oz (225g) small button mushrooms	4 cups small button mushrooms
1¼ pints (700ml) milk	3 cups milk
2 oz (55g) 81 per cent wholemeal flour	2 ounces 81 per cent wholewheat flour
½ teaspoon ground mace *or* nutmeg	½ teaspoon ground mace *or* nutmeg
½ teaspoon ground mustard powder	½ teaspoon ground mustard powder
1 oz (30g) polyunsaturated margarine	2 tablespoons polyunsaturated margarine
Sea salt and freshly ground black pepper	Sea salt and freshly ground black pepper
4 oz (115g) finely grated farmhouse Cheddar cheese	1 cup finely grated farmhouse Cheddar cheese
¼ pint (140ml) dry white wine	⅔ cup dry white wine

1 Blend the parsley sprigs into the batter (see method opposite), as you add the oil with the motor running.

2 Make pancakes (crêpes) as directed on page 86 and stack one on top of each other until ready to fill.

3 Trim leeks by cutting a slight indent around the area where the coarse leaves begin. Pull off the dark coarse leaves to reveal the lighter green leaves underneath, still attached to the white ends. Wash the leeks well. Cut into ¾ inch (1.5cm) rings.

4 Heat oil in a pan and sauté the leeks for 7 minutes, with the lid on.

5 Set *slicing plate* in position. Wash and wipe the mushrooms. Pack into the feed tube, caps on the outside and slice.

6 Sauté the mushrooms with the leeks for 3 minutes, coating them well with the leek juices. Take off heat and leave to one side.

7 Set *steel blades* in position. Blend half the milk, flour, mace and mustard until smooth. Gradually add the remaining milk and continue to process until well mixed.

8 Heat the margarine in a heavy-based saucepan.

9 Pour in the milk mixture. Bring to boil stirring constantly. Turn down to very low heat and let cook for 2 minutes only. Take off heat.

10 Season with sea salt and freshly ground black pepper. Stir in half the grated cheese.

11 Halve the sauce and stir one half into the leeks and mushrooms.

12 Fill 8 pancakes (crêpes) with 2 tablespoons of the leek mixture, roll each one up and place in a well-greased baking dish. (The remaining 4 pancakes/crêpes may be frozen.)

13 To the remaining sauce add the white wine. Trickle this over the stuffed pancakes (crêpes), leaving the ends free of sauce. Sprinkle over the remaining cheese. Bake at 400°F/200°C (Gas Mark 6) for 20 minutes until golden-brown on top.

Broccoli Pancakes with Spiced Kidney Bean Filling
Makes 10

Imperial (Metric)	American
8 oz (225g) broccoli *or* sprouting broccoli tops	8 ounces broccoli *or* sprouting broccoli tops
4 oz (115g) wholemeal flour	1 cup wholewheat flour
½ teaspoon bicarbonate of soda	½ teaspoon baking soda
8 fl oz (230ml) milk	1 cup milk
1 level teaspoon sea salt	1 level teaspoon sea salt
2 eggs	2 eggs
2 tablespoons sunflower oil	2 tablespoons sunflower oil
4 tablespoons cold water	4 tablespoons cold water
Little soya oil for frying	Little soy oil for frying

For the filling:

Imperial (Metric)	American
6 oz (170g) dry weight red kidney beans, soaked overnight	1 cup dry red kidney beans, soaked overnight
1 dessertspoon clear honey	2 teaspoons clear honey
1 teaspoon sea salt	1 teaspoon sea salt
1 large onion, peeled	1 large onion, peeled
2 tablespoon olive oil	2 tablespoons olive oil
1 quantity Spiced Tomato Sauce (page 69)	1 quantity Spiced Tomato Sauce (see page 69)
3 oz (85g) grated farmhouse Cheddar cheese	¾ cup grated farmhouse Cheddar cheese

1 Cook broccoli in a little salted water for 10 minutes. Drain well and chop. Allow to cool.

2 Set *steel blades* in position. Blend flour, soda, milk, salt, eggs and oil until smooth.

3 Add the chopped broccoli and blend until a green speckled batter is achieved.

4 Pour into a bowl. Cover and leave to stand for 2 hours.

5 Stir in the cold water. The mixture should be a runny batter consistency. Test by taking out 1 tablespoon of the batter, then if it pours off the spoon easily and spreads with a little help from the back of the spoon it is just right. If too thick then add more cold water.

6 Brush a small, heavy-based frying pan with oil. Heat well, then turn down to medium-high, spoon in 2 tablespoons of the mixture and spread thinly to form a circle shape with the back of a spoon. Cook for half a minute, turn over with a palette knife and cook for another half a minute. When cooked, pile on top of each other. They will not stick. Put to one side.

7 Rinse the soaked beans and bring to boil in 1½ pints water. Boil for 10 minutes. Add the honey and simmer for 45 minutes to 1 hour until the beans are soft but not mushy. Add 1 teaspoon sea salt just before the end of cooking time. Drain.

8 Set *steel blades* in position. Chop peeled onion roughly, put into processor bowl and chop finely.

9 Heat oil in a pan. Sauté the onion until soft, about 5 minutes.

10 Stir in the cooked and drained beans, plus half the cold Spiced Tomato Sauce.

11 Cook gently for 10 minutes.

12 Grease a large square or rectangular ovenproof dish. Fill and roll up each pancake (2 tablespoons of the mixture will be ample for each). Place them side by side in the dish.

13 Heat the remaining tomato sauce and trickle this over the pancakes.

14 Then sprinkle on the grated cheese. Bake at 350°F/180°C (Gas Mark 4) for 25 minutes. Serve with a fresh green salad of crisp lettuce, cucumber, watercress and parsley and a lemon and olive oil dressing.

Vegetable Fritters
Makes about 16

If you are making these for children you could leave out the onion and red pepper, but it is best to try them with these vegetables the first time, as I feel children should get used to different flavours.

Imperial (Metric)	American
1 small onion, roughly chopped	1 small onion, roughly chopped
1 small red pepper, roughly chopped	1 small red pepper, roughly chopped
3 oz (85g) wholemeal flour	¾ cup wholewheat flour
1 oz (30g) soya flour	¼ cup soy flour
1 level tablespoon baking powder	1 level tablespoon baking powder
1 large egg	1 large egg
½ teaspoon sea salt	½ teaspoon sea salt
8 fl oz (230ml) milk	1 cup milk
6 oz (170g) frozen sweetcorn, lightly cooked and drained	1 cup frozen sweetcorn, lightly cooked and drained
3 oz (85g) grated Cheddar cheese	¾ cup grated Cheddar cheese
Sunflower oil for frying	Sunflower oil for frying

1 Set *steel blades* in position. Chop onion and red pepper finely. Scoop out and place in a mixing bowl.

2 With steel blades still in position, blend flours, baking powder, egg, salt and milk until smooth.

3 Pour this over the onion and red pepper mixture.

4 Stir in the cooled, cooked sweetcorn and the cheese.

5 Leave to stand for 30 minutes. Stir again.

6 Heat 3 tablespoons oil in a frying pan. Use 1 tablespoon of the mixture for each fritter, spreading them gently with the back of a spoon. Cook 3 at a time. Let them get crisp and golden on one side, using moderate heat for 2 minutes. Toss over with a palette knife and cook for another 2 minutes. Serve with a salad for a very substantial and well-balanced lunch or light supper dish.

Tempura or Pakora

Tempura is the Middle Eastern name for this delightful method of cooking vegetables — Pakora is its Indian equivalent.

The batter can be made more spicy by adding curry powder or chilli powder if you wish. I have only spiced it moderately in the recipe to suit most tastes. It is not strictly a main meal but it would be quite sufficient for a light lunch, as the batter is protein-packed.

Batter

Imperial (Metric)	American
4 oz (115g) gram (chick pea flour)	1 cup garbanzo bean flour
2 oz (55g) soya flour	½ cup soy flour
2 oz (55g) brown rice flour	scant ½ cup brown rice flour
1 level teaspoon coriander powder	1 level teaspoon coriander powder
1 level teaspoon sea salt	1 level teaspoon sea salt
1 level teaspoon baking powder	1 level teaspoon baking soda
⅔ pint (340ml) milk	1½ cups milk
Soya oil for deep frying	Soy oil for deep drying
Raw vegetables*	Raw vegetables*
Shoyu (naturally fermented soya sauce) to serve	Naturally fermented soy sauce to serve

1 Set *steel blades* in position. Blend flours, sea salt, coriander, baking powder and milk until smooth. Pour into a mixing bowl and let stand for 1 hour. Stir before using.

2 Heat oil to very hot as for cooking chips. Dip the vegetables in the batter and deep fry until golden brown. (Watch the oil does not burn; turn it down a little as you fry but still keep it quite hot.) Drain on absorbent kitchen paper.

3 To serve, sprinkle on a little shoyu (soy sauce). Just a few vegetables will make a huge plate of Tempura or Pakora.

*The raw vegetables are a matter of choice. I suggest thin onion rings, thinly sliced potato with skins on, small cauliflower florets, whole small mushrooms, sliced courgettes (zucchini) and aubergines (eggplants). It is best to salt the aubergine (eggplant) slices first — let stand for 30 minutes, rinse and wipe before dipping into the batter.

Wholemeal Pastry Case
Will fill a 10 inch/25cm flan case

Making pastry with wholemeal flour can be a little tricky unless you release the gluten in the flour and break down the coarser grain. To do this I use a creaming, rather than the rubbing-in, method. I also knead the dough for a few minutes. This process seems to lighten wholemeal pastry considerably. I also use a little baking powder, but this is not essential. I sometimes add 2 ounces (55g) grated cheese to the pastry for a more savoury taste.

Imperial (Metric)	American
4 oz (115g) polyunsaturated margarine	½ cupful polyunsaturated margarine
3 tablespoons cold water	3 tablespoons cold water
8 oz (225g) wholemeal flour	2 cups wholewheat flour
½ teaspoon sea salt	½ teaspoon sea salt
1 very level teaspoon baking powder (optional)	1 very level teaspoon baking soda (optional)

1 Set *steel blades* in position. Cream margarine, water, and 3 tablespoons flour until smooth.

2 Add salt, baking powder and the remaining flour gradually, with the motor still running. Process until the mixture forms small balls. Take out and knead for about 1½ minutes. Place in a plastic bag and chill in the fridge for 30 minutes.

3 Roll out on a lightly-floured surface. For best results place a see-through plastic sheet on top of the pastry as you roll it out. Slide a palette knife underneath, curl one edge onto the rolling pin and lift onto a greased flan dish. Trim off edges. Bake blind at 375°F/190°C (Gas Mark 5) for 10 minutes.

Leek filling:

Imperial (Metric)	American
8 oz (225g) leeks, when trimmed	8 ounces leeks, when trimmed
2 tablespoons olive or sunflower oil	2 tablespoons olive or sunflower oil
4 eggs, beaten	4 eggs, beaten
7 fl oz (200ml) milk	¾ cupful milk
3 tablespoons spray-dried skimmed milk powder	3 tablespoons spray-dried skimmed milk powder
2 tablespoons thick natural yogurt	2 tablespoons thick plain yogurt
I level teaspoon dried tarragon	I level teaspoon dried tarragon
¼ teaspoon mustard powder	¼ teaspoon mustard powder
¼ teaspoon freshly ground black pepper	¼ teaspoon freshly ground black pepper
½ teaspoon sea salt	½ teaspoon sea salt
4 oz (115g) grated farmhouse Cheddar cheese	I cup grated farmhouse Cheddar cheese

1 Wash leeks and cut into ½ inch (1cm) rings. Heat oil in a pan and sauté the leeks on moderate heat for 10 minutes with lid on. Cool.

2 Set *steel blades* in position. Put all remaining ingredients except the cheese into the processor bowl. Blend until well mixed.

3 Sprinkle half the grated cheese on the bottom of the cooked pastry case. Spoon on the cooled leeks. Pour over the egg mixture. Top with the remaining cheese.

4 Bake in a pre-heated oven, 375°F/190°C (Gas Mark 5), for 35 to 40 minutes, until slightly risen and set. Let stand for 5 minutes before serving.

Broccoli filling:

Use the same liquid, spice and herb ingredients as for the leek filling, but instead of leeks chop 8 ounces (225g) of lightly steamed broccoli and spoon this over the first layer of cheese. Also, use crumbled Leicester or Caerphilly cheese instead of the grated farmhouse Cheddar.

Pepper and mushroom filling:

Follow the recipe for leek filling, but sauté 1 small chopped onion for 5 minutes, add 6 ounces (170g) sliced mushrooms instead of the leeks and sauté for 3 minutes. Use oregano instead of tarragon and top with thin rings of red and green pepper, slightly overlapping. Finally sprinkle on the remaining cheese. Bake in the same way.

Ratatouille Pie

A lovely dish, hot or cold. It is topped with wholemeal breadcrumbs and grated cheese which gives a nice crisp layer to seal in the flavour.

Imperial (Metric)	American
1 large onion, peeled	1 large onion, peeled
2 medium courgettes	2 medium zucchini
1 large green pepper (or ½ red, ½ green)	1 large green pepper (or ½ red, ½ green)
3 tablespoons olive oil	3 tablespoons olive oil
2 cloves garlic	2 cloves garlic
14 oz (395g) tin tomatoes, well-drained and chopped	14 ounce can tomatoes, well-drained and chopped
1 tablespoon tomato purée	1 tablespoon tomato paste
1 teaspoon basil	1 teaspoon basil
1 bay leaf	1 bay leaf
Sea salt and freshly ground black pepper	Sea salt and freshly ground black pepper
3 eggs, beaten	3 eggs, beaten
4 oz (115g) grated Cheddar cheese	4 ounces grated Cheddar cheese
1 recipe wholemeal pastry case, baked blind, see page 93	1 recipe wholewheat pastry case, baked blind, see page 93
2 oz (55g) wholemeal breadcrumbs	2 ounces wholewheat breadcrumbs

1 Set *slicing plate* in position. Cut onion in quarters lengthwise and slice in an upright position. Scoop out.

2 Cut courgettes (zucchini) in half lengthwise and pack into the tube in an upright position. Slice. Scoop out.

3 Cut pepper in quarters lengthwise and slice in an upright position.

4 Heat oil in a heavy-based saucepan. Sauté onion and garlic for 10 minutes with lid on.

5 Add the courgettes (zucchini) and peppers and continue to cook for another 10 minutes with the lid on.

6 Stir in the drained tomatoes, tomato purée (paste), basil and bay leaf. Stir. Taste and add sea salt and freshly ground black pepper to taste.

7 Continue to simmer on low heat for 5 more minutes. Allow to cool.

8 Stir in the beaten eggs and half the cheese. Taste again for seasoning, adding more if you wish. Pour into the baked pastry case.

9 Mix the remaining cheese with the breadcrumbs and sprinkle over the top.

10 Bake at 400°F/200°C (Gas Mark 6), for 30 minutes or until the top is golden-brown.

Lentil and Mushroom Pie

You can use aduki beans for this instead of lentils (see page 50 on how to cook).

Imperial (Metric)	American
8 oz (225g) red split lentils	1 cup red split lentils
¾ pint (425ml) water	2 cups water
1 vegetable stock cube	1 vegetable stock cube
1 cinnamon stick	1 cinnamon stick
1 bay leaf	1 bay leaf
1 large onion, peeled	1 large onion, peeled
6 oz (170g) button mushrooms	3 cups button mushrooms
2 tablespoons sunflower oil	2 tablespoons sunflower oil
3 large tomatoes, skinned and chopped	3 large tomatoes, skinned and chopped
2 tablespoons lemon juice	2 tablespoons lemon juice
1 teaspoon coriander	1 teaspoon coriander
½ teaspoon freshly ground black pepper	½ teaspoon freshly ground black pepper
1 tablespoon tomato purée	1 tablespoon tomato paste
2 tablespoons fresh chopped parsley	2 tablespoons fresh chopped parsley
1 egg, beaten	1 egg, beaten
1½ times the wholemeal pastry recipe, see page 93, using 12 oz (340g) flour, plus 3 oz (85g) grated cheese added to the dough	1½ times the wholewheat pastry recipe, see page 93, using 3 cups flour, plus ¾ cup grated cheese added to the dough
A little beaten egg, for glazing	A little beaten egg, for glazing

1 Wash lentils by placing in a sieve and letting cold water run over them for a minute.

2 Place in a saucepan with the water, stock cube, cinnamon stick and bay leaf. Bring to boil and let simmer with the lid on for 15 to 20 minutes. The water should all be absorbed. If not, drain off excess. Remove cinnamon stick and bay leaf.

3 Set *steel blades* in position. Cut onion lengthwise and slice in an upright position. Scoop out.

4 Slice mushrooms, caps to the outside of the feed tube.

5 Heat oil in a pan; sauté the onion on moderate heat until golden. Add the mushrooms and continue to fry for 3 minutes. Stir in the tomatoes, lemon juice, coriander, black pepper and tomato purée (paste). Cook for 2 minutes more.

6 Stir in the parsley. Let mixture completely cool before adding the beaten egg.

7 Line a pastry case with half the pastry. Fill this with the lentil mixture. Cover the top with the other half of the pastry. Prick all over, crimp the edges and brush with a little beaten egg. Bake at 400°F/200°C (Gas Mark 6) for 40 minutes.

3.

SALADS, DRESSINGS AND LIGHT VEGETABLE DISHES

Dressings and salads

The higher percentage of raw, fresh vegetables and fruit you eat, the healthier you will be. Many of my students have said to me at the beginning of my cookery courses that they are not too keen on salads or fruit. In fact, the vast majority had salads twice a week on average with the occasional apple and orange. For most of them it just needed a little stimulation of the taste buds, with delicious dressings poured over crisp, fresh vegetables and fruit, to encourage them to eat more of these valuable foods which are high in fibre, well supplied with vitamins and minerals and low in calories.

Advocates of a 'raw food' diet tell us that approximately 50 to 70 per cent of our diet should be uncooked. Well, although I secretly agree, a good start would be to make sure that you and those you feed have at least one good salad daily. The best way to ensure this is to make one or two jars of dressing at the beginning of the week. Half the work is done with these in the fridge. The rest is easy, a little chopping or shredding and you have a wholesome bowlful.

I always use cold-pressed oils for dressings (see notes on fats, page 10) and cider vinegar or lemon juice. Cider vinegar helps maintain the balance between the acids and the alkalis in the body, as well as containing a wealth of minerals. It is important to prepare salads just before serving and toss in a dressing as soon as the vegetables and fruit are cut. This holds in valuable nutriments, especially the elusive vitamin C which is destroyed soon after exposure to the atmosphere.

We are fortunate to have such an abundant choice of fresh vegetables and fruit available in our shops from home and abroad, but I try to buy what is in season as much as possible. Why buy limp, tasteless lettuces in winter when there is home-grown white and red cabbage and, of course, Chinese leaf from abroad to choose from? These store extremely well if wrapped in containers and refrigerated.

You can concoct a salad from a huge variety of vegetables and fruit, but care is needed to blend those which complement each other. I've eaten many a salad that has been a painful, jaw-aching experience. Yes, definitely good for you — but let these beautiful fresh foods be not only healthy but taste their exquisite best.

One of my favourite ingredients in salads is home-grown or bought bean sprouts. I cannot praise them enough. They are high in protein and rich in the C and B vitamins. Because they are such a marvellous food, of which you can have a constant supply, I cannot resist putting the recipe for growing your own in all my cookbooks. (See page 112 for recipe.) Bean sprouts are also delicious in sandwiches with cheese or pâté because they remain crisp. A handful added to your stir-fried vegetables for just one minute before the end of cooking time will give a fresh crispness to the finished dish.

Two salad dressings to store

As previously mentioned, having a dressing ready is a great encouragement to preparing a salad. I will give you my two basic dressings which I keep permanently in the fridge. These need only a few extra ingredients added to alter their flavour for individual recipes. For example, to a basic mayonnaise, which is quite delicious on a potato salad, I simply blend in red pepper, capers, some horseradish root and natural yogurt. The resulting dressing is pink in colour and has a piquant flavour which will add an exotic touch to bean or cabbage salad. For this kind of recipe you will find your processor invaluable.

The recipes will state any extras to the basic dressings where needed, as well as giving you a variety of more unusual dressings such as Tofu Avocado on page 117.

French Dressing

You can use all lemon juice instead of vinegar and lemon to achieve a lighter-tasting dressing or use all vinegar for a stronger sharp flavour. Double the recipe will fill a 1 pound (455g) honey jar.

Imperial (Metric)	American
6 tablespoons olive oil *or* cold pressed safflower *or* sunflower oil	6 tablespoons olive oil *or* cold pressed safflower *or* sunflower oil
1 tablespoon fresh lemon juice	1 tablespoon fresh lemon juice
1 tablespoon cider vinegar	1 tablespoon cider vinegar
¼ teaspoon dry mustard powder	¼ teaspoon dry mustard powder
¼ teaspoon freshly ground black pepper	¼ teaspoon freshly ground black pepper
½ teaspoon sea salt	½ teaspoon sea salt
¼ teaspoon clear honey	¼ teaspoon clear honey
1 small clove garlic, crushed	1 small clove garlic, crushed

1 With *steel blades* in position process together until the mixture emulsifies. If making enough to store, refrigerate but take out 10 minutes before using and shake well.

Mayonnaise

Imperial (Metric)	American
8 fl oz (200ml) cold-pressed sunflower oil	I cup cold-pressed sunflower oil
I egg	I egg
I egg yolk	I egg yolk
½ teaspoon dry mustard powder	½ teaspoon dry mustard powder
¼ teaspoon freshly ground black pepper	¼ teaspoon freshly ground black pepper
½ teaspoon sea salt	½ teaspoon sea salt
2 tablespoons lemon juice *or* lemon juice and cider vinegar	2 tablespoons lemon juice *or* lemon juice and cider vinegar

1 With *steel blades* in position, place 2 tablespoons of the oil, the egg, egg yolk, mustard, pepper, salt and lemon juice into the processor bowl. Blend for 1 minute.

2 Very gradually trickle the remaining oil into the feed tube with the motor still on. The mixture will thicken when you have put about three-quarters of the oil in. Trickle the rest in and it will continue to thicken. Store in a screw top jar in the fridge.

Salads

Summer Green Salad

In summer I use Cos, Webb's or any fresh green lettuce. (In winter my favourite is lamb's lettuce: small, crisp and full of flavour but, unfortunately, not often commercially available.) Lettuce will make a salad on its own with a French dressing, or you can add various green salad vegetables as suggested in this recipe. In the list of ingredients I state watercress or nasturtium leaves. These are both slightly hot salad greens. I put the watercress as a first choice only because this is more easily available unless you grow nasturtiums.

Imperial (Metric)	American
I fresh lettuce	I fresh lettuce
Handful young spinach leaves	Handful young spinach leaves
I bunch watercress *or* handful nasturtium leaves	I bunch watercress *or* handful nasturtium leaves
6 spring onions	6 scallions
½ large cucumber	½ large cucumber

For the herb dressing:

Imperial (Metric)	American
I quantity French dressing (see page 99)	I quantity French dressing (see page 99)
½ oz (15g) parsley sprigs	½ ounce parsley sprigs
¼ oz (8g) mint leaves	¼ ounce mint leaves
I level teaspoon dried tarragon or 2 sprigs fresh	I level teaspoon dried tarragon or 2 sprigs fresh

1 Wash lettuce well in plenty of cold water. Leave the leaves whole except the extra large ones. Dry on absorbent kitchen paper.

2 Wash spinach leaves in the same way and pat dry.

3 Wash watercress or nasturtium leaves and break off small sprigs.

4 Trim spring onions (scallions), leaving as much green on as possible. Slice into thin rings.

5 Wash cucumber and cut in half lengthwise. With *slicing plate* in position, place cucumber in the feed tube in an upright position, press down with pusher and slice. Scoop out.

6 With *steel blades* in position, pour the French dressing into the processor bowl and add the washed parsley and mint sprigs and the tarragon. Blend for a few seconds.

7 Arrange lettuce, spinach and watercress on a platter or shallow serving bowl. Sprinkle over the spring onions (scallions). Arrange cucumber slices overlapping around the edge of the salad leaves and in a circle in the centre. Pour over the prepared dressing and serve immediately.

Winter Green Salad with Poached Carrots

For the avocado dressing:

Imperial (Metric)	American
I quantity French dressing (page 99)	I quantity French dressing (page 99)
½ large avocado	½ large avocado
2 tablespoons thick natural yogurt	2 tablespoons thick plain yogurt

For the salad:

Imperial (Metric)	American
8 oz (225g) carrots	8 ounces carrots
½ cucumber	½ cucumber
I crisp eating apple	I crisp eating apple
4 spring onions	4 scallions
I medium head Chinese leaf	I medium head Chinese leaf
I punnet mustard and cress	I punnet mustard and cress
2 tablespoons fresh chopped parsley	2 tablespoons fresh chopped parsley

1 Set *steel blades* in position. Blend French dressing, avocado and yogurt until smooth and a thick creamy consistency. Scoop out and rinse out processor bowl.

2 Wash and scrape carrots. Set *slicing plate* in position. Stand carrots in feed tube in an upright position. Slice.

3 Boil carrots in a little salted water for 3 minutes only. Drain and toss immediately in a little of the prepared dressing. Cool.

4 Cut cucumber and apple into small chunks. Trim spring onions (scallions), leaving as much green on as possible. Cut into thin rings.

5 Toss cucumber, apple and spring onions (scallions) with the cooled carrots, adding a little more dressing.

6 Cut Chinese leaf in half lengthwise, then widthwise into lengths to fit snugly into the feed tube. Still with *slicing plate* in position, slice. The Chinese leaf will be in thin slivers.

7 Wash mustard cress and mix this with the shredded Chinese leaf. Pour over the remaining dressing and toss.

8 Place Chinese leaf and cress in a large shallow serving bowl and spoon over the carrot mixture. Sprinkle the parsley over the top to garnish.

Butter Bean and Cauliflower with Pepper and Tomato Vinaigrette

Imperial (Metric)	American
4 oz (115g) butter beans	⅔ cup Lima beans
Sea salt	Sea salt
I small cauliflower, broken into small florets	I small cauliflower, broken into small florets

For the pepper and tomato vinaigrette:

Imperial (Metric)	American
¼ pint (140ml) French dressing (see page 99)	⅔ cup French dressing (see page 99)
½ small green pepper, de-seeded and roughly chopped	½ small green pepper, de-seeded and roughly chopped
I level teaspoon tomato purée	I level teaspoon tomato paste
I level teaspoon dried basil *or* a few fresh sprigs	I level teaspoon dried basil *or* a few fresh sprigs

1 Wash beans and soak overnight, changing the water three times. Cook in fresh water, boiling vigorously for 10 minutes then bubbling gently for approximately 40 minutes. Watch the beans, as these cook into a mush quite easily. Add a little sea salt 10 minutes before the end of cooking time. Drain and let cool.

2 Cook cauliflower in a little salted boiling water for 3 minutes only. Drain and mix with cooked beans.

3 Set *steel blades* in position and put French dressing, green pepper, tomato purée (paste) and basil into the processor bowl. Blend together until smooth.

4 Pour over the beans and cauliflower, tossing well. Let stand to marinate, turning with a fork a few times, for 1 hour or more.

Potato Salad in the Pink

Imperial (Metric)	American
2 lbs (900g) potatoes (new are best)	2 pounds potatoes (new are best)
4 sticks celery	4 stalks celery
I pickled dill cucumber	I pickled dill cucumber
I small onion	I small onion
4 oz (II5g) frozen peas	⅔ cup frozen peas
3 tablespoons fresh chopped parsley	3 tablespoons fresh chopped parsley

For the pink dressing:

Imperial (Metric)	American
⅓ pint (200ml) mayonnaise (see page 100)	¾ cup mayonnaise (see page 100)
½ red pepper, de-seeded and roughly chopped	½ red pepper, de-seeded and roughly chopped
I level tablespoon capers	I level tablespoon capers

1 Scrub potatoes and steam until cooked but still firm. (Only peel if using old potatoes.) Dice.

2 Set *slicing plate* in position. Cut celery into lengths just under the height of feed tube. Pack upright into feed tube and slice.

3 Slice dill cucumber by standing upright in the tube.

4 Scoop out and fork celery and cucumber carefully into the potatoes.

5 Chop the small onion very finely (it will be too small to chop on steel blades) and fork into the potato mixture.

6 Cook peas in boiling salted water for 4 minutes only.

7 Fork these, with 2 tablespoons of the parsley, into the other vegetables.

8 Set *steel blades* in position and blend the mayonnaise, red pepper and capers until smooth and pink.

9 Carefully fork the dressing into the vegetables, taking care not to break up the potatoes. Garnish with 1 tablespoon chopped parsley. If you have any red pepper left you could decorate the top with 3 thin rings slightly overlapping in the centre, plus the parsley.

Chick Pea and Olive Salad

Imperial (Metric)	American
4 oz (115g) dry weight chick peas	¾ cup dry garbanzo beans
10 black olives, stoned	10 black olives, pitted
I quantity French dressing, made with olive oil (see page 99)	I quantity French dressing, made with olive oil (see page 99)
6 firm tomatoes	6 firm tomatoes
½ green and ½ red pepper	½ green and ½ red pepper
4 oz (115g) small button mushrooms	2 cups small button mushrooms
I small onion, peeled	I small onion, peeled
2 bunches watercress	2 bunches watercress
2 hard-boiled eggs	2 hard-boiled eggs
I tablespoon fresh chopped mint leaves *or* parsley	I tablespoon fresh chopped mint leaves *or* parsley

1 Wash chick peas (garbanzo beans) and pick over for stones. Soak for 12 hours, changing the water three times. Rinse and cook in fresh water for 1 hour, or until soft. (Add 1 teaspoon sea salt 10 minutes before end of cooking time.) Drain well.

2 Place in a bowl with the olives and half of the French dressing.

3 Cut tomatoes into thin wedges and fork gently into the chick peas (garbanzo beans).

4 Set *slicing plate* in position and place red, then green, pepper upright in feed tube and slice.

5 Wash and wipe mushrooms and put in feed tube, caps to the outside, and slice. Fork into the chick pea (garbanzo bean) mixture.

6 Slice onion into very thin rings and reserve for garnish.

7 Wash watercress and break off into small sprigs.

8 To assemble the salad, spread watercress on the bottom of a shallow dish. Spoon over the chick pea (garbanzo bean) mixture. Slice the cold hard-boiled eggs, garnish the top with these and the onion rings. Pour over the remaining French dressing and sprinkle on the mint or parsley. Serve on whole crisp lettuce leaves.

Raw Beetroot with Yogurt Apple Mint Dressing

Imperial (Metric)	American
1½ lbs (680g) raw beetroot	1½ pounds raw beets
½ medium fennel root	½ medium fennel root
1 tablespoon olive oil	1 tablespoon olive oil
Pinch sea salt	Pinch sea salt
8 lettuce leaves	8 lettuce leaves

For the yogurt apple mint dressing:

Imperial (Metric)	American
¾ pint (425ml) natural yogurt (dripped through muslin for 1 to 2 hours)	2 cups plain yogurt (dripped through muslin for 1 to 2 hours)
2 eating apples	2 eating apples
1 large clove garlic, crushed	1 large clove garlic, crushed
2 tablespoons lemon juice	2 tablespoons lemon juice
1 teaspoon clear honey	1 teaspoon clear honey
1 tablespoon chopped mint leaves	1 tablespoon chopped mint leaves
Sea salt and freshly ground black pepper	Sea salt and freshly ground black pepper
1 teaspoon chopped mint, to garnish	1 teaspoon chopped mint, to garnish

1 Peel beetroot (beets) with a potato peeler, rinse and cut in quarters.

2 Set *shredding plate* in position. Stack beets horizontally into feed tube. Shred.

3 Cut fennel into chunks and pack into feed tube and shred. Wash out processor bowl.

4 Mix beetroot (beets) and fennel in a bowl with 1 tablespoon olive oil and a good pinch of sea salt. Cover and set aside.

5 Wash lettuce and pat dry on absorbent kitchen paper. Put in a plastic bag and refrigerate until needed.

6 Scrape off yogurt from the muslin and put in a bowl. It should be the consistency of mayonnaise.

7 Set *steel blades* in position. Peel off a very thin skin from the apples. Core and roughly chop. Place in the processor bowl with the garlic, lemon juice, honey and mint. Blend until smooth.

8 Stir the apple purée into the yogurt. Taste and add sea salt and freshly ground black pepper to taste.

9 Assemble the salad by spreading the lettuce leaves on a large platter. Spoon the beetroot (beets) and fennel mixture piled high on each leaf. Make an indent in each pile and spoon the yogurt sauce into the centre of each. Sprinkle a little fresh mint over the top to garnish. Very special, cooling and delicious.

Note: Do not add yogurt to the apples when blending in the machine or you will get a very runny sauce. Just stir the apple purée into the yogurt as directed. This way it will remain reasonably thick.

Spinach Salad with Féta Cheese and Orange

Imperial (Metric)	American
8 oz (225g) spinach leaves, well washed and chopped	8 ounces spinach leaves, well washed and chopped
2 oranges, peeled and cut in small triangular chunks	2 oranges, peeled and cut in small triangular chunks
4 tomatoes, cut in small chunks	4 tomatoes, cut in small chunks
I celery heart (save outer sticks for another dish)	I celery heart (save outer stalks for another dish)
I medium onion	I medium onion
8 oz (225g) Féta cheese	8 ounces Féta cheese
I quantity French dressing (see page 99)	I quantity French dressing (see page 99)
I tablespoon capers (optional)	I tablespoon capers (optional)

1 Spread spinach on a large serving dish.

2 Arrange the chopped orange and tomato on the leaves.

3 Set *slicing plate* in position. Cut celery heart in two widthwise then stand the two pieces upright in the feed tube. Slice.

4 Cut onion in half and stand each half upright in the feed tube. Slice.

5 Sprinkle the celery and onion over the orange and tomato chunks.

6 Crumble on the Féta cheese.

7 Pour over the dressing and finally garnish with the capers.

Saffron Rice Salad with Toasted Pumpkin Seeds

Imperial (Metric)	American
I large onion, peeled	I large onion, peeled
2 tablespoons cold-pressed sunflower oil	2 tablespoons cold-pressed sunflower oil
I large clove garlic, crushed	I large clove garlic, crushed
8 oz (225g) short grain brown rice	I cupful short grain brown rice
I pint (570ml) hot water plus I vegetable stock cube	2½ cups hot water plus I vegetable stock cube
Pinch saffron *or* I level teaspoon turmeric	Pinch saffron *or* I level teaspoon turmeric
4 oz (115g) frozen peas	⅔ cup frozen peas
4 oz (115g) frozen sweetcorn	⅔ cup frozen sweetcorn
I red or green pepper	I red or green pepper
¼ pint (140ml) French dressing (see page 99)	⅔ cup French dressing (see page 99)
2 tablespoons sultanas	2 tablespoons golden seedless raisins
A little shoyu (naturally fermented soya sauce) to taste	A little naturally fermented soy sauce to taste
2 oz (55g) pumpkin seeds	⅓ cup pumpkin seeds
Sprigs of parsley to garnish	Sprigs of parsley to garnish

1 Set *slicing plate* in position. Cut onion in quarters lengthwise. Pack, 2 quarters at a time, side by side, into the feed tube and slice.

2 Heat oil in a heavy-based, medium-sized saucepan. Sauté onion and garlic for 10 minutes.

3 Wash rice by placing in a sieve and running cold water over it for 30 seconds. Drain well. Stir rice with the onion and fry gently for 4 minutes. Add the hot water, stock cube and saffron *or* turmeric.

4 Bring to boil, turn down to simmer and cook with a tight lid on for 30 minutes. The rice will absorb all the water.

5 Cook peas and sweetcorn in a little salted boiling water for 4 minutes only. Drain.

6 With *slicing plate* in position, cut red or green pepper in quarters and pack, standing upright, into the feed tube. Slice.

7 When rice is cooked (drain off any moisture), fork in the corn, peas, pepper, sultanas (golden seedless raisins) and French dressing.

8 Toast the pumpkin seeds by placing in a thick, dry frying pan over moderate heat. Stir with a wooden spoon until lightly browned. Do not burn. Fork these into the rice mixture, leaving a few on top. Garnish with sprigs of parsley.

Kohlrabi, Onion and Tomato Salad

Imperial (Metric)	American
I lb (455g) kohlrabi, thinly peeled	I pound kohlrabi, thinly peeled
2 medium onions, peeled	2 medium onions, peeled
A little cider vinegar	A little cider vinegar
Sea salt and freshly ground black pepper	Sea salt and freshly ground black pepper
6 firm tomatoes	6 firm tomatoes
¼ pint (140ml) French dressing (see page 99)	⅔ cup French dressing (see page 99)
I teaspoon dried basil *or* a few chopped fresh sprigs	I teaspoon dried basil *or* a few chopped fresh sprigs

1 Set *slicing plate* in position. Cut kohlrabi in halves. Place each half upright in the feed tube and slice thinly.

2 Blanch the kohlrabi in boiling water for 1 minute only. Drain and toss in 2 tablespoons of the French dressing. Cover and put aside.

3 Cut onions in half and slice each half thinly, standing upright in the feed tube.

4 Put onions in a bowl and pour over a little cider vinegar, sea salt and black pepper. Let marinate for 1 hour at least. This softens the onions. Drain off vinegar.

5 Slice tomatoes in thin rings.

6 Assemble the salad by mixing the onions with the kohlrabi. Spread out on a shallow salad dish. Place tomato rings on top. Pour over the remaining dressing and sprinkle the basil over this.

Tabbouleh (Bulgur Wheat Salad) with Pine Kernels

This salad is delicious served with thick natural yogurt or cottage cheese. You can add many other vegetables to the bulgur if you wish.

Imperial (Metric)	American
8 oz (225g) bulgur wheat	8 ounces bulgur wheat
2 tablespoons shoyu (naturally fermented soya sauce)	2 tablespoons naturally fermented soy sauce
1 onion, small to medium, peeled	1 onion, small to medium, peeled
1 oz (30g) parsley sprigs	1 ounce parsley sprigs
½ oz (15g) mint sprigs	½ ounce mint sprigs
6 firm tomatoes, cut in small wedges	6 firm tomatoes, cut in small wedges
3 tablespoons olive *or* safflower oil	3 tablespoons olive *or* safflower oil
3 tablespoons lemon juice	3 tablespoons lemon juice
2 cloves garlic, peeled and chopped	2 cloves garlic, peeled and chopped
1 very level teaspoon ground coriander	1 very level teaspoon ground coriander
½ very level teaspoon ground cumin	½ very level teaspoon ground cumin
½ teaspoon freshly ground black pepper	½ teaspoon freshly ground black pepper
1 tablespoon shoyu (naturally fermented soya sauce)	1 tablespoon naturally fermented soy sauce
2 oz (55g) pine kernels	⅓ cup pine kernels
1 bunch watercress, to garnish	1 bunch watercress, to garnish

1 Soak the bulgur in enough boiling water to cover it by 1 inch (2.5cm). Add 1 tablespoon shoyu (soy sauce). Cover and let stand for 20 to 30 minutes (no cooking is required).

2 Set *steel blades* in position. Roughly chop the onion and place in the processor bowl, with parsley and mint sprigs. Finely chop. Scoop out. Fork this into the chopped tomatoes.

3 With steel blades still in position put oil, lemon juice, garlic, ground coriander, ground cumin, black pepper and the rest of the shoyu (soy sauce) into the processor bowl and blend until it emulsifies.

4 Pour this over the tomato mixture and then fork the dressing and vegetables into the prepared bulgur wheat.

5 Fork in the pine kernels, leaving a few on top. Garnish with sprigs of watercress.

Note: You can use buckwheat (see page 76 on how to cook) as a wholesome and very tasty alternative to bulgur in this recipe.

Flageolet Beans with Tofu and Avocado Vinaigrette

Imperial (Metric)	American
12 oz (340g) flageolet beans	1½ cups flageolet beans

For the tofu and avocado vinaigrette:

Imperial (Metric)	American
2 oz (55g) piece of tofu	¼ cup tofu
½ medium avocado	½ medium avocado
I clove garlic, crushed	I clove garlic, crushed
I tablespoon olive oil	I tablespoon olive oil
2 tablespoons lemon juice	2 tablespoons lemon juice
I teaspoon Dijon mustard	I teaspoon Dijon mustard
½ teaspoon clear honey	½ teaspoon clear honey
Sea salt and freshly ground black pepper to taste	Sea salt and freshly ground black pepper to taste

1 Wash beans and pick over for stones. Soak overnight. Change the water three times. Rinse. Bring to boil, boil for 5 minutes and then simmer for 40 minutes or until soft. Add a little sea salt 10 minutes before the end of cooking time. Drain and put in a serving bowl.

2 Set *steel blades* in position. Blend all the tofu and avocado vinaigrette ingredients except the salt and pepper, together until smooth. Pour into a small bowl. Season with sea salt and freshly ground black pepper and stir into the warm beans. Marinate for a few hours, stirring occasionally to coat the beans well.

Bean Sprouts with Sweet and Sour Dressing

You can buy bean sprouts very cheaply but, even better, you can grow your own easily from a variety of seeds. The protein content varies depending on the seeds used, but they are all rich in the B and C vitamins. Mung beans are the most commonly sprouted and contain 37 per cent protein. Other seeds, such as aduki bean and whole lentils, containing 25 per cent protein, also sprout easily. Alfalfa seeds, high on the list nutritionally, containing 40 per cent protein, are thin and light in texture like mustard and cress, but quite different in flavour. Wholewheat sprouts are very sweet and are great added to your bread recipes (see page 160).

To sprout your own, take just 1 heaped tablespoon of seeds, wash well and pick over for stones. Leave to soak in cold water for 2 hours. Drain and place in a glass jar. Put a piece of muslin over the opening and secure with an elastic band. Rinse the seeds three times daily, letting the water drain out through the muslin. Keep the jar in a warm place, but not in direct sunlight. A room temperature of 60 to 65°F (18°C) is about right. The time seeds take to sprout varies, but usually it's 3 to 5 days.

The following recipe makes a large bowlful of hearty fresh goodness.

Imperial (Metric)	American
12 oz (340g) bean sprouts	12 ounces bean sprouts
6 oz (170g) small button mushrooms	3 cups small button mushrooms
1 small green pepper, de-seeded	1 small green pepper, de-seeded
1 small red pepper, de-seeded	1 small red pepper, de-seeded
2 medium carrots, scraped	2 medum carrots, scraped
1 ripe peach *or* ½ mango, when in season (optional)	1 ripe peach *or* ½ mango, when in season (optional)
A little fresh chopped parsley to garnish	A little fresh chopped parsley to garnish

For the sweet and sour dressing:

Imperial (Metric)	American
4 tablespoons cold-pressed sesame, safflower *or* sunflower oil	4 tablespoons, cold-pressed sesame, safflower *or* sunflower oil
1 tablespoon cider vinegar	1 tablespoon cider vinegar
1 tablespoon shoyu (naturally fermented soya sauce)	1 tablespoon naturally fermented soy sauce
1 teaspoon clear honey	1 teaspoon clear honey
¼ teaspoon mustard powder	¼ teaspoon mustard powder
Good pinch of ground five spice *or* allspice	Good pinch of ground five spice *or* allspice
1 heaped teaspoon freshly grated ginger	1 heaped teaspoon freshly grated ginger
1 large clove garlic, crushed	1 large clove garlic, crushed

1 Rinse bean sprouts and pat dry on absorbent kitchen paper. Put in a salad bowl.

2 Wash and pat dry the mushrooms. Set *slicing plate* in position. Pack mushrooms, caps to the outside, into the feed tube and slice.

3 Cut peppers in half lengthwise and stand each half upright in the feed tube. Slice.

4 Stand carrots upright in the feed tube (if thick, cut in half lengthwise before slicing). Slice.

5 Scoop out sliced vegetables and fork into the bean sprouts. Rinse out processor bowl.

6 Cut peach or mango into small pieces and add to salad bowl, leaving them as near the surface as possible.

7 Set *steel blades* in position and blend all the dressing ingredients together until it emulsifies. Add more honey if you like a sweeter taste.

8 Pour over the salad vegetables and finally sprinkle on the parsley.

Crunchy Winter Salad with Pecan Nuts

For the horseradish mayonnaise dressing:

Imperial (Metric)	American
¼ pint (140ml) Mayonnaise (see page 100)	⅔ cup Mayonnaise (see page 100)
2 tablespoons horseradish root	2 tablespoons horseradish root
2 tablespoons thick natural yogurt	2 tablespoons thick plain yogurt

For the salad:

Imperial (Metric)	American
½ small white cabbage	½ small white cabbage
I small onion, peeled	I small onion, peeled
4 sticks celery	4 stalks celery
I crisp eating apple	I crisp eating apple
2 medium carrots, scraped	2 medium carrots, scraped
2 level tablespoons sultanas	2 level tablespoons golden seedless raisins
2 oz pecan nuts	½ cup pecan nuts
A little fresh chopped parsley to garnish	A little fresh chopped parsley to garnish

1 Set *steel blades* in position. Blend mayonnaise, horseradish and yogurt. Place in a small bowl. Clean out processor bowl.

2 Trim off dead outer leaves of the cabbage. Wash well and cut into wedges to fit feed tube. Stand cabbage upright in the tube and slice, keeping moderate pressure on the pusher.

3 Set *slicing plate* in position. Drop whole small onion into tube and slice. Scoop out and place in a salad bowl. Toss with a little of the dressing. Set slicing plate back into position. Cut celery in lengths to fit feed tube. Pack upright into the tube and slice.

4 Quarter apple and core. Place 2 quarters at a time side by side into feed tube and slice. Scoop out and toss with the cabbage, adding a little more dressing.

5 Set *shredding plate* in position. Cut carrots into 2½ inch (6cm) lengths and stack horizontally into the feed tube. Push firmly with the pusher and shred. Scoop out and add this with the sultanas (golden seedless raisins) and most of the pecan nuts to the cabbage mixture. Stir in the rest of the dressing. Garnish with the parsley and a few pecan nuts.

Black-eye Beans with Apricot and Ginger Dressing

Imperial (Metric)	American
12 oz (340g) dried black-eye beans	1½ cups dried black-eye beans
6 fresh chillies, chopped	6 fresh chilies, chopped
1 teaspoon sea salt	1 teaspoon sea salt

For the apricot and ginger dressing:

I use fresh apricots for this recipe, but you can use dried. Choose the full-flavoured apricot pieces. Wash well and soak in water with a heaped teaspoon of clear honey overnight. Cook for 10 minutes until most of the liquid is evaporated.

Imperial (Metric)	American
6 oz (170g) fresh apricots *or* 2 oz (55g) dried	6 ounces fresh apricots *or* 2 ounces dried
1 heaped teaspoon clear honey	1 heaped teaspoon clear honey
2 tablespoons olive oil	2 tablespoons olive oil
1 tablespoon cider vinegar	1 tablespoon cider vinegar
1 teaspoon fresh ginger, grated	1 teaspoon fresh ginger, grated
2 cloves garlic, chopped	2 cloves garlic, chopped
1 tablespoon shoyu (naturally fermented soya sauce)	1 tablespoon naturally fermented soy sauce

1 Wash beans and pick over for stones. Soak overnight, changing the water three times. Rinse.

2 Set *steel blades* in position. Blend chopped chillies with ½ pint (285ml/1⅓ cups) water until you have a pulp.

3 Put beans, chilli pulp and 1½ pints (850ml/3¾ cups) water in a saucepan. Bring to boil and cook, with lid on, for approximately 45 minutes or until soft but not mushy. Add 1 teaspoon sea salt 10 minutes before the end of cooking time. Drain, place in a serving bowl.

4 Wash, stone and cook fresh apricots in a very little water with the honey. Cook until soft and most of the water has evaporated. With *steel blades* in position, blend apricots, olive oil, vinegar, ginger, garlic and shoyu (soy sauce) until smooth. Stir into the warm beans and marinate for a few hours or overnight.

Note: Delicious with vegetable curry, see page 80, instead of Dhal or with a fresh green salad and pitta bread (see page 161 for recipe).

Continental Lentil Salad

Imperial (Metric)	American
8 oz (225g) continental green lentils	I cup split peas
I pint (570ml) cold water, slightly salted	2½ cups cold water, slightly salted
3 sticks celery	3 stalks celery
4 oz (115g) button mushrooms	2 cups button mushrooms

For the tomato sauce dressing:

Imperial (Metric)	American
I small onion, peeled	I small onion, peeled
2 tablespoons olive oil	2 tablespoons olive oil
I large clove garlic, crushed	I large clove garlic, crushed
6 fresh, ripe tomatoes	6 fresh, ripe tomatoes
½ small green pepper, roughly chopped	½ small green pepper, roughly chopped
I very level teaspoon marjoram *or* basil	I very level teaspoon marjoram *or* basil
I small bay leaf	I small bay leaf
I tablespoon chopped parsley	I tablespoon chopped parsley
Freshly ground black pepper to taste	Freshly ground black pepper to taste
Sea salt to taste	Sea salt to taste
½ teaspoon cayenne pepper (Optional. Use only if you want a slightly fiery taste)	½ teaspoon cayenne pepper (Optional. Use only if you want a slightly fiery taste)
2 tablespoons lemon juice	2 tablespoons lemon juice
A little chopped parsley to garnish	A little chopped parsley to garnish

1 Wash lentils and pick over for stones. Bring to boil in the water. Let simmer with lid on for 30 minutes. Watch to see that they do not overcook. Drain well. Let cool.

2 Set *slicing plate* in position. Cut celery into lengths to fit feed tube. Stand upright in tube and slice. Wash and pat dry the mushrooms. Pack into feed tube, caps to the outside. Slice.

3 Fork into the cold lentils.

4 Halve the onion and stand upright in feed tube. Slice.

5 Heat oil in a heavy-based, medium-sized saucepan.

6 Sauté onion and garlic for 7 minutes.

7 Skin tomatoes by steeping in boiling water for a few minutes, then peel.

8 Set *steel blades* in position and place tomatoes, green pepper and marjoram into the processor bowl. Blend until fairly smooth.

9 Pour this over the onion and garlic. Add the bay leaf, parsley, black pepper, sea salt, cayenne (if used) and lemon juice. Bring to boil and let simmer for 20 minutes. When cold, stir into the lentil mixture. Sprinkle on a little chopped parsley to garnish.

Stuffed Courgettes (Zucchini) with Mushroom and Lemon Cream Sauce

Imperial (Metric)	American
4 medium courgettes	4 medium zucchini
3 tablespoons cold-pressed sunflower oil *or* butter	3 tablespoons cold-pressed sunflower oil *or* butter
Sea salt and freshly ground black pepper to taste	Sea salt and freshly ground black pepper to taste
2 tablespoons lemon juice	2 tablespoons lemon juice
I lb (455g) button mushrooms	I pound button mushrooms
I slightly rounded tablespoon 81 per cent wheatmeal flour	I slightly rounded tablespoon 81 per cent wheatmeal flour
¼ pint (140ml) soured cream	⅔ cup sour cream
I tablespoon chopped parsley	I tablespoon chopped parsley
Pinch cayenne pepper	Pinch cayenne pepper
2 tablespoons freshly grated Parmesan cheese (optional)	2 tablespoons freshly grated Parmesan cheese (optional)

1 Wash the courgettes (zucchini), trim off stalks and blanch in boiling water for 2 minutes only. Drain. Wipe and cut in half lengthwise. Scoop out a shallow groove in each half (reserving the pulp).

2 Arrange the courgettes (zucchini) hollow side up in a lightly-oiled ovenproof dish. Brush with 1 tablespoon of the oil. Sprinkle with a little sea salt and freshly ground black pepper and 1 tablespoon lemon juice. Cover the dish tightly. Bake in centre of the oven, 350°F/180°C (Gas Mark 4), for 25 minutes.

3 Wash and wipe the mushrooms. Set *slicing plate* in position, pack mushrooms into the feed tube, caps to the outside. Slice.

4 Heat remaining oil in a heavy-based pan. Sauté the mushrooms for 1 minute, tossing them as you fry. Sprinkle with a little sea salt and black pepper. Cook for 2 more minutes.

5 Sprinkle the flour over the mushrooms and stir briskly with a wooden spoon to blend in well. Gradually stir in the cream, stirring continuously until it thickens. Take off heat.

6 Set *steel blades* in position. Put parsley, cayenne and courgette (zucchini) pulp into the processor bowl. Blend to a purée.

7 Stir the purée into the mushroom mixture and cook very gently for 1 to 2 minutes more. Take off heat. Stir in the remaining 1 tablespoon lemon juice.

8 Spoon this mixture into the baked courgette (zucchini) cases. These are delicious without the cheese but, if you prefer, sprinkle the Parmesan cheese on top and grill until very light golden-brown.

Variation:

Courgettes (Zucchini) Stuffed with Nut and Seed Pâté

Prepare the courgettes (zucchini) as in the previous recipe but do not bake them. Purée the pulp and mix it with a half quantity of the Nut and Seed Pâté, see page 32. Spoon the mixture into the blanched courgette (zucchini) halves. Pour over 1 pint (570ml/2½ cups) thick white sauce. Sprinkle on a little grated cheese and bake, tightly covered, for 20 minutes at 350°F/180°C (Gas Mark 4). Uncover and bake for 10 more minutes. This is a very substantial main meal for 4 or a starter for 8.

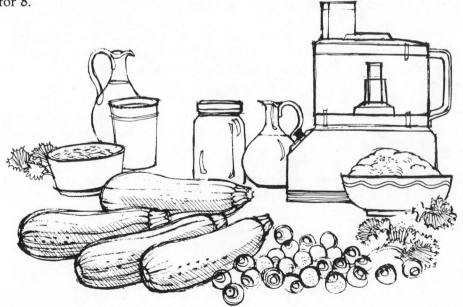

Stuffed Peppers with Rice and Pine Kernels
Serves 4

Imperial (Metric)	American
4 oz (115g) long grain Surinam rice	½ cup long grain Surinam rice
4 medium peppers (red and green mixed, choose squat, not pointed, ones)	4 medium peppers (red and green mixed, choose squat, not pointed, ones)
I medium onion, peeled	I medium onion, peeled
3 tablespoons sunflower *or* olive oil	3 tablespoons sunflower *or* olive oil
2 cloves garlic, crushed	2 cloves garlic, crushed
4 oz (115g) mushrooms	2 cups mushrooms
I tablespoon parsley, chopped	I tablespoon parsley, chopped
I large sprig mint, chopped	I large sprig mint, chopped
I level teaspoon coriander seeds, crushed	I level teaspoon coriander seeds, crushed
4 large ripe tomatoes	4 large ripe tomatoes
I tablespoon tomato purée	I tablespoon tomato paste
I tablespoon lemon juice	I tablespoon lemon juice
3 oz (85g) pine kernels	⅓ cup pine kernels
Sea salt and freshly ground black pepper	Sea salt and freshly ground black pepper
2 oz (55g) grated Cheddar *or* Parmesan cheese	½ cup grated Cheddar *or* Parmesan cheese

1 Wash rice well by placing in a sieve and running cold water over it for 1 minute.

2 Bring to boil in double its volume of cold salted water, turn down to simmer and let cook with tight lid on for 25 minutes. (If using Italian long grain rice, instead of Surinam, cook for 35 minutes.) Drain if necessary and leave in a colander until needed.

3 Cut a circle round the top of each pepper to remove the stem and seeds. Place peppers in a pan, cover with boiling water and let stand for 5 minutes. Drain well and put aside.

4 Set *slicing plate* in position. Cut onion in half and pack each half into the feed tube and slice. Scoop out and replace slicing plate.

5 Heat oil in a heavy-based pan. Sauté onion and garlic for 7 minutes.

6 Wash and wipe mushrooms. Pack into feed tube, caps to the outside and slice.

7 Sauté the mushrooms with the onion and garlic for 3 minutes.

8 Add parsley, mint and crushed coriander and continue to cook for 1 minute.

9 Stir cooked rice into the vegetables and, stirring to coat the rice, cook for 1 minute more.

10 Set *steel blades* into position. Skin tomatoes by cutting a small circle round the stem area, blanch in boiling water for 1 to 2 minutes. Peel and roughly chop. Put into processor bowl and blend until thoroughly mashed.

11 Add the mashed tomatoes, tomato purée (paste), lemon juice, pine kernels, sea salt and freshly ground black pepper. Cook for 1 minute.

12 Stand the prepared peppers, open end up, in an oiled ovenproof dish. Spoon in the rice mixture and sprinkle on the grated cheese.

13 Spoon 2 tablespoons water into the dish and bake just above the centre of the oven, 350°F/180°C (Gas Mark 4), for 35 to 40 minutes.

Aubergines (Eggplants), Turkish Style
Serves 6 as an appetizer

These are mouth-watering and very more-ish. Great as a starter or served with cottage cheese as a lunch or supper dish. Another way to serve these as a main meal is to top with slices of Mozzarella cheese and grill to melt cheese only, but not to brown. (As a main meal it will serve 3.)

Imperial (Metric)	American
3 medium to large aubergines, about 10 oz (285g) each in weight	3 medium to large eggplants, about 10 ounces each in weight
Sea salt and freshly ground black pepper	Sea salt and freshly ground black pepper
Olive oil	Olive oil
3 medium onions (about 1 lb/455g when peeled)	3 medium onions (about 1 pound when peeled)
1 large clove garlic, crushed	1 large clove garlic, crushed
12 oz (340g) soft ripe tomatoes	12 ounces soft ripe tomatoes
1 very level teaspoon ground cinnamon	1 very level teaspoon ground cinnamon
2 tablespoons chopped parsley	2 tablespoons chopped parsley
2 tablespoons shelled pistachios, cut in half (optional)	2 tablespoons shelled pistachios, cut in half (optional)

1 Cut the stalks off the aubergines (eggplants). Wash and put them in a large saucepan. Pour boiling water over them. Cover and let stand for 10 minutes. Drain and plunge in cold water for 5 minutes. Drain again.

2 Cut in half lengthwise and scoop out pulp, leaving ½ inch (1.5cm) thick outer 'shell'. Set pulp aside until needed.

3 Place aubergine (eggplant) shells in an oiled ovenproof dish (no cover needed). Sprinkle with a little sea salt and black pepper. Pour 2 teaspoons of olive oil into each shell and bake in the centre of the oven at 350°F/180°C (Gas Mark 4) for 30 minutes.

4 Set *slicing plate* in position and cut onions in half lengthwise. Pack each half into feed tube and slice.

5 Heat 3 tablespoons olive oil in a heavy-based pan. Sauté onion and garlic for 5 minutes until soft.

6 Skin tomatoes by cutting a small circle round the stalk end. Blanch in boiling

water for 1 to 2 minutes. Peel. Set *steel blades* in position. Chop the tomatoes on a low speed to the count of 5 only. Add tomatoes, cinnamon and parsley to the onions and cook, uncovered, on gentle heat for 20 minutes. The juice will then be reduced by half.

7 Chop the aubergine (eggplant) pulp and add this, with the pistachios, to the tomato and onion mixture and continue to cook for 10 minutes more.

8 Spoon this mixture into the cooked aubergine (eggplant) shells. Can be eaten hot or cold.

Nutty Cauliflower with Lemon Dill Sauce
Serves 4

Imperial (Metric)	American
I large cauliflower	I large cauliflower
Half quantity of Nut and Seed Pâté, see page 33	Half quantity of Nut and Seed Pâté, see page 33

For the lemon dill sauce:

Imperial (Metric)	American
I oz (28g) unbleached white flour	¼ cup unbleached white flour
¼ pint (140ml) milk	⅔ cup milk
¼ pint (140ml) stock (if no fresh stock, use water and ¼ vegetable stock cube)	⅔ cup stock (if no fresh stock, use water and ¼ vegetable stock cube)
I oz polyunsaturated margarine	I ounce polyunsaturated margarine
I tablespoon dried dill	I tablespoon dried dill
Sea salt and freshly ground black pepper	Sea salt and freshly ground black pepper
2 tablespoon lemon juice	2 tablespoons lemon juice
I teaspoon very finely grated lemon rind	I teaspoon very finely grated lemon rind

1 Cut off outer tough leaves and thick stalk base of the cauliflower (leave on as much green as possible), and wash well.

2 Cook in boiling salted water for 10 to 12 minutes until tender. Drain and keep warm.

3 For the sauce, set *steel blades* in position, place flour, cold milk, cold stock, margarine and dill in the processor bowl. Blend until smooth. Add sea salt and black pepper.

4 Oil a heavy-based saucepan. Pour in the sauce batter and bring to boil on moderate heat, stirring constantly. Let cook gently for 3 minutes only. Take off heat, stir in the lemon juice and rind.

5 Heat the nut and seed pâté very gently on low heat.

6 To assemble the dish, place cauliflower in a shallow serving bowl. Ease apart the florets, taking care not to break them. Stuff in the nut and seed pâté between the florets. Trickle over the lemon sauce, letting some of the colourful pâté show through.

Pizza Sauce
Enough to top 2 large Pizzas

You will find a recipe for Pizza dough on page 164 in the chapter on yeasted dough. This sauce is also delicious on pasta or stirred into rice for risotto.

Imperial (Metric)	American
2 medium onions, peeled and roughly chopped	2 medium onions, peeled and roughly chopped
2 cloves garlic, crushed	2 cloves garlic, crushed
3 sticks celery, roughly chopped	3 stalks celery, roughly chopped
3 tablespoons sunflower or olive oil	3 tablespoons sunflower or olive oil
½ red and ½ green pepper	½ red and ½ green pepper
4 oz (115g) button mushrooms	2 cups button mushrooms
I teaspoon basil	I teaspoon basil
I large bay leaf	I large bay leaf
I lb 12 oz (795g) tin tomatoes, chopped	3½ cups canned tomatoes, chopped
2 tablespoons tomato purée	2 tablespoons tomato paste
I level teaspoon herb or sea salt	I level teaspoon herb or sea salt
Freshly ground black pepper	Freshly ground black pepper

1 Set *steel blades* in position. Put onion, garlic and celery into the processor bowl. Chop.

2 Heat oil in a heavy-based saucepan. Sauté the finely chopped onion, garlic and celery for 5 minutes until soft.

3 Set *slicing plate* in position. Cut pepper through the centre lengthwise. Pack into the feed tube in an upright position and slice. Wash and wipe mushrooms and pack into the feed tube, caps to the outside. Slice.

4 Add peppers, mushrooms, basil and bay leaf and continue to cook for 5 minutes.

5 Stir in the tomatoes and tomato purée. Taste and add the herb or sea salt and freshly ground black pepper to your own taste. Cook for a further 20 minutes until the juice from the tomatoes has reduced. If the sauce is runny, then either ladle out a little and use in soup or add a little bran to thicken.

Leeks with Yogurt and Tarragon Sauce
Serves 4

Imperial (Metric)	American
6 large leeks	6 large leeks
¾ pint (420ml) water	2 cups water
I very level teaspoon sea salt	I very level teaspoon sea salt
½ teaspoon freshly ground black pepper	½ teaspoon freshly ground black pepper
½ teaspoon fennel seeds	½ teaspoon fennel seeds
I large clove garlic, crushed	I large clove garlic, crushed
A few sprigs parsley	A few sprigs parsley
I bay leaf	I bay leaf

For the sauce:

Imperial (Metric)	American
½ pint (285ml) natural yogurt	1⅓ cups plain yogurt
3 egg yolks	3 egg yolks
I dessertspoon lemon juice	2 teaspoons lemon juice
½ teaspoon mustard powder	½ teaspoon mustard powder
½ teaspoon dried tarragon	½ teaspoon dried tarragon
Sea salt and freshly ground black pepper	Sea salt and freshly ground black pepper

1 Trim off coarse leaves from the leeks. Slit them to 2 inches (5cm) from the start of the white end. Wash thoroughly.

2 Put water, salt, black pepper, fennel seeds, garlic, parsley and bay leaf in a saucepan. Bring to boil and simmer for 10 minutes. Strain off liquid.

3 Cook leeks in the broth for 10 minutes or until tender. Leave to marinate in the liquid while you make the sauce.

4 Set *steel blades* in position. Put yogurt, egg yolks, lemon juice, mustard powder and tarragon into the processor bowl. Blend for ½ minute. Pour into a *Pyrex* bowl and season with salt and freshly ground black pepper. Place the bowl over a pan of gently simmering water. Cook, stirring constantly, until it thickens, approximately 15 minutes.

5 Drain leeks and either leave whole or cut into 2-inch (5cm) chunks. Arrange in a serving dish and pour over the sauce. Garnish with a little more tarragon or parsley. (Reserve the broth to use as stock.)

Variation:

Broccoli with Yogurt and Tarragon Sauce

Instead of leeks use broccoli florets, but cook 1 onion in the broth before straining.

Pepper Stew
Serves 4

This is delicious served hot with bean burgers or cold as a starter.

Imperial (Metric)	American
I large Spanish onion, peeled	I large Spanish onion, peeled
3 tablespoons olive *or* sunflower oil	3 tablespoons olive *or* sunflower oil
2 cloves garlic, crushed	2 cloves, garlic, crushed
2 large green peppers	2 large green peppers
2 large red peppers	2 large red peppers
I level teaspoon marjoram	I level teaspoon marjoram
I small bay leaf	I small bay leaf
I lb (455g) ripe, fresh skinned *or* tinned tomatoes, chopped	I pound ripe, fresh skinned *or* canned tomatoes, chopped
2 tablespoons shoyu (naturally fermented soya sauce)	2 tablespoons naturally fermented soy sauce
I level teaspoon clear honey	I level teaspoon clear honey
2 tablespoons lemon juice	2 tablespoons lemon juice
Dash Tabasco sauce	Dash Tabasco sauce

1 Set *slicing plate* in position. Cut onion lengthwise in quarters. Fit snugly in an upright positon into feed tube and slice. Scoop out and replace plate.

2 Heat oil in a large, heavy-based saucepan. Sauté onion and garlic for 10 minutes.

3 Cut peppers in quarters lengthwise. Pack into the feed tube in an upright position. Slice.

4 Add these to the onion and garlic and continue to cook for 5 minutes.

5 Add all the other ingredients and let simmer gently, for 20 minutes, until the juice from the tomatoes has evaporated. Serve hot or cold.

4.

DESSERTS AND PUDDINGS

Your food processor really does lots of the work for you in this chapter. It will save you time spent on hand-whisking, chopping and blending and will help you produce so many delicious and wholesome treats.

Most of us feel like something sweet on occasions, or maybe you have a particularly sweet tooth and crave sweet dishes more often. Unfortunatley, the majority of desserts are not only overladen with sugar (sucrose) but also contain too much saturated fat, both of which, when overeaten, can be detrimental to your health. (See notes on sugar and fats, page 10.)

However, you can make delicious, rich-tasting desserts with the minimum amount of ingredients which bump up the calories and raise the level of cholesterol in the blood. But here I feel moderation is the keynote to enjoyably healthy eating. A little of what you fancy is alright only if most of the time you eat a balanced wholesome diet. For instance, I would serve my Swiss Yogurt Cheesecake (page 142) after a light meal which included a generous fresh salad; whereas, if lasagne were the main dish, I would follow this with a seasonal fruit salad and yogurt honey cream. Make your fruit salad more exciting by adding mango or kiwi fruit when available. Let the fruit marinate in fresh fruit juice, to which you could add a tablespoon of Grand Marnier or cherry brandy for special occasions.

My favourite ingredients in making desserts are fresh fruit, dried fruit and yogurt. Another ingredient I include is fructose (fruit sugar) which is absorbed more slowly from the intestinal tract than sucrose (ordinary sugar) and therefore does not cause blood-sugar levels to rise as sharply. It looks like castor sugar but is a third sweeter so you use less. Apple juice concentrate is another great sweetener, especially in pies or poured over pancakes instead of maple syrup. When making sweet pies, tarts or crumbles use wholemeal flour, adding just a little unbleached white for extra light pastry. If milk, eggs or cream are the main ingredients in your sweet dessert then avoid these items in the rest of the menu.

You will note, when making jellies, fruit mousses or fluffs, that I used *Gelozone* instead of gelatine. *Gelozone* is made from vegetable gums, whereas gelatine is produced by boiling animal bones and cartilage.

Mixed Dried Fruit Mousse

Imperial (Metric)	American
2 oz (55g) each of dried prunes, figs, apricots and apples	⅓ cup each of dried prunes, figs, apricots and apples
I pint (570ml) boiling water	2½ cups boiling water
10 oz (285ml) natural yogurt	1⅓ cups plain yogurt
2 teaspoons *Gelozone*	2 teaspoons *Gelozone*
2 rounded tablespoons Barbados sugar *or* 3 tablespoons apple juice concentrate	2 rounded tablespoons Barbados sugar *or* 3 tablespoons apple juice concentrate
2 tablespoons double cream (optional)	2 tablespoons heavy cream (optional)
A few toasted almonds or walnuts to decorate	A few toasted almonds or walnuts to decorate

1 Wash dried fruit well and soak overnight or for a few hours in the boiling water.

2 Cook fruit gently for 10 minutes only. Drain and retain ½ pint (285ml/1⅓ cups) of the liquid, plus 4 extra tablespoons.

3 Remove prune stones (pits) and set *steel blades* in position. Blend fruit and 4 tablespoons of the liquid to a smooth purée. Cool.

4 Stir in the yogurt and set aside.

5 Mix *Gelozone* and sugar with a little of the liquid until smooth then gradually add the rest of the liquid.

6 Bring slowly to boil, stirring constantly, and simmer for 2 to 3 minutes only. Cool.

7 Stir into the fruit purée.

8 Whip cream and fold into the mixture. Spoon into individual dishes and decorate with the chopped toasted almonds or walnuts.

Apricot and Ginger Mousse
Serves 4 to 5

You can either use bottled stem ginger which is soaked in syrup or, as I prefer, fresh grated ginger root. Try to get unsulphured apricots which are dark in colour and naturally dried. (For children use 1 rounded teaspoon cinnamon instead of ginger.)

Imperial (Metric)	American
I pint (570ml) boiling water	2½ cups boiling water
8 oz (225g) dried apricot pieces, well washed	1½ cups dried apricot pieces, well washed
1½-inch (4cm) knob fresh ginger *or* 3 pieces of stem ginger	1½-inch knob fresh ginger *or* 3 pieces of stem ginger
2 teaspoons *Gelozone*	2 teaspoons *Gelozone*
4 rounded tablespoons dried skimmed milk powder	4 rounded tablespoons dried skimmed milk powder
2 oz (55g) Barbados sugar	⅓ cup Barbados sugar
I large egg, separated	I large egg, separated
Toasted chopped hazelnuts to decorate	Toasted chopped hazelnuts to decorate

1 Pour the boiling water over the washed apricots and let soak overnight or for a few hours.

2 Drain and retain liquid, making it up to 1 pint (570ml/2½ cups) by adding extra cold water.

3 Thinly peel and finely grate the fresh ginger.

4 Put apricots, ginger and half the liquid into a heavy-bottomed saucepan and cook gently for 8 minutes.

5 Set *steel blades* in position and blend until smooth. Clean and dry processor bowl.

6 Mix *Gelozone*, milk powder and sugar (or apple juice concentrate) together. Blend to a smooth paste with a little of the remaining liquid and then gradually add the rest.

7 Bring slowly to the boil and cook for 2 to 3 minutes.

8 Remove from heat and stir into the apricot purée.

9 Blend in the egg yolk and leave to cool.

10 Set *egg white whisk* in position and whisk egg white until stiff.

11 Fold into the apricot mixture and spoon into individual dishes.

12 Sprinkle with toasted chopped hazelnuts. Chill for at least 2 hours.

Carob and Orange Mousse
Serves 4 to 5

A rich dessert for special occasions only. Carob powder is very similar to drinking chocolate powder, but is caffeine free and naturally sweet.

Imperial (Metric)	American
1 tablespoon carob powder	1 tablespoon carob powder
2 teaspoons *Gelozone*	2 teaspoons *Gelozone*
Juice of 2 oranges plus water to make up	Juice of 2 oranges plus water to make up
¾ pint (425ml) liquid	2 cups liquid
1 tablespoon Grand Marnier (optional)	1 tablespoon Grand Marnier (optional)
Rind of 1 orange	Rind of 1 orange
2 eggs, separated	2 eggs, separated
2 tablespoons fruit sugar	2 tablespoons fruit sugar
¼ pint (140ml) double cream, lightly whipped	⅔ cup heavy cream, lightly whipped

1 Blend carob powder and *Gelozone* to a smooth paste with a little of the water and orange juice liquid, gradually adding the rest of the liquid including the Grand Marnier, if used. Add rind.

2 Bring to boil slowly, stirring constantly, and simmer for 3 minutes. Let cool until just warm.

3 Set *steel blades* in position and blend egg yolks with the fruit sugar until thick and creamy. Pour into a bowl and pour the warm carob liquid over the beaten yolk. Fold together. Allow to cool and stiffen slightly. Clean and dry processor bowl.

4 Set *egg white whisk* in position and whisk egg whites until stiff.

5 Fold the lightly whipped cream, then the stiffly beaten egg whites into the carob mixture. Spoon into individual glasses and chill until set.

Yogurt and Nectarine Ice Cream

This recipe requires a rich custard made with yogurt, sour cream and eggs. To prevent the yogurt from curdling it is important to cook it slowly with the eggs in a pan over hot — not boiling — water, preferably in a double boiler.

You can use ripe peaches or apricots for this recipe instead of nectarines. Skin the peaches or apricots by dipping in boiling water before peeling.

Imperial (Metric)	American
¾ pint (425ml) thick natural yogurt	2 cups thick plain yogurt
½ pint (285ml) sour cream (2 small cartons)	1⅓ cups sour cream
2 eggs plus 2 egg yolks	2 eggs plus 2 egg yolks
3 tablespoons clear honey	¼ cup clear honey
1 lb (455g) ripe nectarines	4 cups ripe nectarines
2 cardamom seeds (optional)	2 cardamom seeds (optional)
A few drops natural vanilla essence	A few drops natural vanilla essence

1 Set *steel blades* in position. Put yogurt, sour cream, eggs, egg yolks and honey in the processor bowl and blend.

2 Put this into a double boiler over hot, not boiling, water. Stir until the mixture thickens and coats the back of the spoon. Let cool. Clean and dry bowl.

3 Wash fruit, slice in half and take out stone, then roughly chop.

4 With *steel blades* in position, mash fruit.

5 Split the cardamoms and crush the seeds as finely as possible.

6 Stir the seeds, a few drops of vanilla essence and the fruit into the cooled custard.

7 Freeze in a suitable container and place in the fridge approximately 25 minutes before serving.

Variation:

Yogurt and Raspberry Ice Cream

Use the same ingredients and follow the same method as for Yogurt and Nectarine Ice Cream, but substitute raspberries for the nectarines. Purée raspberries, then sieve to remove seeds; 12 oz (340ml/3 cups) raspberries will be enough to give a full fruity taste. You can use strawberries in exactly the same way. Adding 1 tablespoon Kirsh to the fruit purée makes it perfect for special occasions.

Hazelnut Ice Cream

This recipe is a quick, easy and healthy treat, using low-fat curd cheese or *fromage blanc* which is low in calories, slightly sharp and refreshing.

Imperial (Metric)	American
3 oz (85g) hazelnuts	¾ cup hazelnuts
1 lb (455g) low-fat curd cheese or *fromage blanc*	2 cups low-fat curd cheese or *fromage blanc*
4 tablespoons apple juice concentrate	4 tablespoons apple juice concentrate
2 tablespoons clear honey	2 tablespoons clear honey

1 Toast hazelnuts in the oven, 350°F/180°C (Gas Mark 4), for 20 minutes. Chop roughly and leave aside.

2 Set *steel blades* in position and put curd cheese or *fromage blanc,* apple juice concentrate and honey into the processor bowl. Blend together until smooth.

3 Stir in the chopped toasted nuts.

4 Pour into a plastic container and freeze.

5 Take out 25 minutes before serving so that the ice cream is firm but not too hard.

Note: Serve with fresh fruit salad or soft fruits when in season. Sliced fresh peaches marinated in a little apple juice concentrate and freshly grated ginger is a real treat with this ice cream for special occasions.

Pecan Nut Ice Crunch

Simple to prepare and an absolute winner with all who have tasted this crunchy cooler. You can use almonds or hazelnuts, which are a bit cheaper than pecans.

Imperial (Metric)	American
3 oz (85g) pecan nuts	¾ cup pecan nuts
3 oz (85g) wholewheat flakes, crushed	2 cups wholewheat flakes, crushed
3 egg whites	3 egg whites
3 oz (85g) fruit sugar *or* Barbados sugar	½ cup fruit sugar *or* Barbados sugar
2 tablespoons skimmed milk powder	2 tablespoons skimmed milk powder
½ pint (250ml) natural yogurt	1⅓ cups plain yogurt

1 Set *steel blades* in position. Grind nuts very briefly. They should be like a breadcrumbs, not a powdery consistency.

2 Put on a baking sheet and toast under the grill (broiler) for 1 to 2 minutes only. Do not burn. Let cool. Clean out bowl.

3 Mix crushed flakes with the toasted nuts.

4 Set *egg white whisk* in position and whisk egg whites until stiff. Take out and gradually hand whisk in the sugar.

5 Stir milk powder into the yogurt.

6 Fold the flakes, nuts and yogurt into the egg whites.

7 Put this mixture into a suitable container with a tight lid and freeze until quite firm. Take out 25 minutes before serving to soften the mixture. Delicious with a fresh fruit or dried fruit salad.

Apple, Mint and Carob Chip Fluff
Serves 4 to 5

Imperial (Metric)	American
3 large cooking apples, thinly peeled and cored	3 large cooking apples, thinly peeled and cored
4 large sprigs mint	4 large sprigs mint
2 tablespoons water	2 tablespoons water
3 level tablespoons clear honey	3 level tablespoons clear honey
7 fl oz (200ml) natural yogurt	1 cup plain yogurt
2 egg whites	2 egg whites
3 tablespoons carob *or* chocolate chips	3 tablespoons carob *or* chocolate chips

1 Cut apples into chunks. Set *steel blades* in position and finely chop apple. Clean and dry bowl.

2 Break off the tops of the sprigs of mint and set aside for decoration.

3 Heat water and honey in a heavy-bottomed saucepan.

4 Add mint sprigs and apple and cook gently for 5 minutes until soft and mushy. Take out mint and set aside to cool.

5 Stir in yogurt.

6 Set *egg white whisk* in position and whisk egg whites until stiff.

7 Fold into the apple mixture with the carob or chocolate chips, then spoon into individual serving dishes. Chill well and decorate with the tops of the mint sprigs.

Redcurrant Fool

You can use blackcurrants but I prefer redcurrants for this recipe as they are not so sharp. Fresh apricots are also delicious.

Imperial (Metric)	American
12 oz (350g) redcurrants	3 cups redcurrants
Juice of ½ lemon	Juice of ½ lemon
2 rounded tablespoons clear honey	2 rounded tablespoons clear honey
½ pint (275ml) water	1⅓ cups water
2 tablespoons *Gelozone*	2 tablespoons *Gelozone*
½ pint (275ml) thick natural yogurt	1⅓ cups thick plain yogurt

1 Place redcurrants, lemon juice, honey and half the water in a heavy-bottomed saucepan. Bring to boil and simmer gently for 3 minutes.

2 Mix *Gelozone* to a smooth paste with the remaining water.

3 Mix into redcurrants and boil for 2 minutes, stirring constantly.

4 Set *steel blades* in position and purée the cooked redcurrants until smooth. Let cool.

5 Fold in the yogurt. Spoon into individual serving dishes and chill until set.

Fruit Brulée
Serves 4 to 5

For this recipe you can use many different fruits. I prefer fresh apricots, plums or blackcurrants.

Imperial (Metric)	American
3 oz (85g) fruit sugar	½ cup fruit sugar
6 tablespoons water	6 tablespoons water
12 oz (340g) fresh apricots, plums *or* blackcurrants	12 ounces fresh apricots, plums *or* blackcurrants
2 level teaspoons arrowroot plus 1 tablespoon cold water	2 level teaspoons arrowroot plus 1 tablespoon cold water
1 small carton sour cream (approx. 5 fl oz/140ml)	⅔ cup sour cream
1 rounded tablespoon soft raw cane sugar mixed with ½ teaspoon ground cinnamon for caramel topping	1 rounded tablespoon soft raw cane sugar mixed with ½ teaspoon ground cinnamon for caramel topping

1 Put sugar and water into a heavy-bottomed saucepan. Heat until sugar has dissolved.

2 Add fruit and cook until tender, no more than 5 minutes.

3 Blend arrowroot with the tablespoon cold water until smooth and add to fruit. Boil for 1 minute more.

4 Set *steel blades* in position and blend fruit until smooth.

5 Spoon fruit into individual small flame-proof dishes. Spread top with a thin layer of sour cream and sprinkle on the soft brown sugar and cinnamon.

6 Set under a hot grill (broiler) for a few seconds just until sugar bubbles and caramelizes.

Chilled Mango Cheese Pie
6 slices

This pie takes 24 hours to set, so it is best to prepare the day before needed. This fills a 9 inch (23cm) pie or loose-bottomed tin. I use Ricotta cheese which is made from sheep's milk and is low in fat.

For the base:

Imperial (Metric)	American
6 oz (170g) wholewheat digestive biscuits	6 ounces wholewheat digestive biscuits
2 oz (55g) sesame seeds	⅓ cup sesame seeds
½ teaspoon ground cinnamon	½ teaspoon ground cinnamon
3 oz (85g) melted polyunsaturated margarine	⅓ cup melted polyunsaturated margarine

For the filling:

Imperial (Metric)	American
8 oz (225g) Ricotta cheese, roughly crumbled	2 cups Ricotta cheese, roughly crumbled
6 oz (170g) natural yogurt	1 cup natural yogurt
3 tablespoons clear honey	¼ cup clear honey
3 drops natural vanilla essence	3 drops natural vanilla essence
Finely grated rind of ½ lemon	Finely grated rind of ½ lemon
1 ripe mango *or* 2 large ripe peaches	1 ripe mango *or* 2 large ripe peaches
1 oz (28g) flaked toasted almonds	¼ cup flaked toasted almonds

To make the base:

1 Set *steel blades* in position. Break biscuits up roughly and put into the processor bowl with sesame seeds and cinnamon. Process until mixture resembles fine breadcrumbs.

2 Scoop out into a mixing bowl and fork in the melted margarine.

3 Press evenly into the well-greased tin and bake at 300°F/150°C (Gas Mark 2) for 5 minutes only. Leave to get completely cold.

For the filling:

1 Set *steel blades* in position. Put Ricotta cheese, yogurt, honey, vanilla essence and lemon rind into the processor bowl and blend together until smooth.

2 Peel mango and cut into small thin slivers. Leave 5 slices aside for garnish. (If using peaches, dip in hot water then peel.)

3 Stir mango slices into the cheese mixture.

4 Pour into the prepared biscuit crust. Decorate the centre of the filling with the five slices forming a flower shape and sprinkle on the toasted almonds.

5 Chill for 24 hours.

Notes: For special occasions you could marinate the mango *or* peaches in a little brandy, apple juice concentrate and freshly grated ginger root overnight. Drain and add as above. Reserve the juice and serve separately to those who wish to spoon it on to their individual serving.

Baked Apples with Fig and Aniseed

Imperial (Metric)	American
8 dried figs, trimmed	8 dried figs, trimmed
2 level tablespoons clear honey	2 level tablespoons clear honey
Juice and rind of 1 medium orange	Juice and rind of 1 medium orange
½ teaspoon ground star aniseed	½ teaspoon ground star aniseed
4 large cooking apples, cored	4 large cooking apples, cored

1 Wash figs and soak in a little hot water and honey for a few hours. Roughly chop. Drain and reserve liquid.

2 Set *steel blades* in position and finely chop figs with the orange juice, rind and aniseed (not too mushy).

3 Place apples on a greased, ovenproof dish.

4 Stuff centres with the fig mixture.

5 Bring soaking water to the level of ¼ pint (140ml/⅔ cup).

6 Pour over the apples.

7 Bake at 350°F/180°C (Gas Mark 4) for 45 minutes to 1 hour. Baste apples several times whilst cooking.

Baked Apples with Apricot and Walnut Stuffing

Imperial (Metric)	American
12 dried apricots, well washed *or* 6 oz (170g) apricot pieces	12 dried apricots, well washed *or* just over 1 cup apricot pieces
A little hot water to soak	A little hot water to soak
1 level tablespoon clear honey	1 level tablespoon clear honey
2 level tablespoons apple juice concentrate	2 level tablespoons apple juice concentrate
½ teaspoon ground cinnamon	½ teaspoon ground cinnamon
1 rounded teaspoon freshly grated ginger (optional)	1 rounded teaspoon freshly grated ginger (optional)
2 oz (55g) walnuts, chopped	½ cup English walnuts, chopped
4 large cooking apples, cored	4 large cooking apples, cored

1 Soak apricots in hot water, honey and apple juice concentrate for a few hours or overnight. Drain and reserve the liquid.

2 Set *steel blades* in position and finely chop apricots, with 2 tablespoons soaking water, cinnamon and ginger. Scoop out and stir in the chopped nuts.

3 Place apples on a greased ovenproof dish and stuff centres with the apricot mixture.

4 Bring soaking water to the level of ¼ pint (140ml/⅔ cup) and pour over the apples.

5 Bake at 350°F/180°C (Gas Mark 4) for 45 minutes to 1 hour. Baste apples during cooking time.

Almond Custard

You can use cashew nuts instead of almonds or add 1 tablespoon carob or cocoa powder for a chocolate flavour.

You will need a double layer of muslin for straining the almond milk.

Imperial (Metric)	American
4 oz (115g) almonds	I cup almonds
1½ pints (850ml) skimmed milk *or* soya milk	3¾ cups skimmed milk *or* soy milk
½ oz (15g) polyunsaturated margarine	I tablespoon polyunsaturated margarine
2 tablespoons clear honey	2 tablespoons clear honey
3 tablespoons agar-agar	3 teaspoons agar-agar
A little grated nutmeg	A little grated nutmeg

1 Set *steel blades* in position. Grind almonds as finely as possible then gradually add ½ pint (285ml/1⅓ cups) of the milk through the feed tube while machine is still running.

2 Rub margarine on the base and sides of a medium-sized saucepan.

3 Pour in the almond milk plus the remaining 1 pint (570ml/2½ cups) milk (saving just a little to blend with agar-agar) and let gently simmer for 20 minutes on low heat. Do not boil.

4 Drape the muslin over a colander which you have placed over a bowl. Strain almond milk into this. Squeeze well to extract all the milk. (Use rubber gloves because the liquid will be very hot.)

5 Sweeten with the honey.

6 Blend agar-agar with a little milk until smooth. Pour this into the almond milk, stirring constantly.

7 Re-heat and let gently simmer for 3 more minutes. Pour into individual serving dishes or 1 large serving bowl. Grate a little nutmeg over each serving and chill until set.

Note: Serve with puréed fruit which you have sweetened slightly with apple juice concentrate. Raspberries and strawberries make lovely purées. Raisins soaked in a little lemon juice and honey overnight taste great. Drain and stir 3 ounces (85g) purée into the custard just before chilling.

Swiss Yogurt Cheesecake

This recipe, slightly altered for health reasons, has the same authentic taste of a most delicious cheesecake I tasted 20 years ago in Zurich. Although I was not a professional cook then I loved cooking and had a recipe up my sleeve to exchange with the wonderful chef who gave us this delight. Originally it was made with full cream cheese, all 12 ounces (340g) of it, but I have experimented with this and it has turned out just as good using half-and-half cream cheese and yogurt cheese. For a dish even lower in saturated fat I have tried half-and-half tofu soya cheese (see page 38 for recipe) and yogurt cheese (see page 36 for recipe). This makes a 10-inch (25cm) round cake. Use a spring-form, loose-bottomed cake tin.

Imperial (Metric)	American
I biscuit base (see page 138 for recipe)	I biscuit base (see page 138 for recipe)

For the filling:

Imperial (Metric)	American
8 oz (225g) cream cheese *or* tofu	1⅓ cups cream cheese *or* tofu
8 oz (225g) yogurt cheese	1⅓ cups yogurt cheese
3 oz (85g) fruit sugar (or less)	½ cup fruit sugar (or less)
4 eggs, separated	4 eggs, separated
4 drops pure vanilla essence	4 drops pure vanilla essence
Juice of ½ lemon	Juice of ½ lemon
Rind of I lemon (very finely grated)	Rind of I lemon (very finely grated)
A little sour cream, for topping	A little sour cream, for topping
Strawberries, raspberries or fresh, lightly cooked apricots, to decorate	Strawberries, raspberries or fresh, lightly cooked apricots, to decorate

1 Prepare the biscuit base, as on page 138, and leave to cool.

2 Set *steel blades* in position. Cream the cheese *or* tofu, yogurt cheese and fruit sugar until smooth. Add egg yolks one at a time while motor is still on.

3 Add vanilla essence, lemon juice and rind. Blend for 10 more seconds.

4 Scoop out and put in a mixing bowl. Wash and dry processor bowl well.

5 Set *egg white whisk* in position and whisk the egg whites until stiff.

6 Scoop out and fold into the cheese mixture with a metal spoon. Do not whisk in. Fold gently, popping the bubbles gently as you do so. The mixture should be light and frothy.

7 Pour this into the prepared cold biscuit base.

8 Bake at 325°F/170°C (Gas Mark 3) in the centre of the oven for 1 hour. Cover with a piece of greaseproof paper or foil if it is browning too much after 40 minutes.

9 Leave in the oven to cool down after cooking. (Letting the cake cool in the warm oven stops the cake from caving in.) Allow it to get cold before decorating the top.

10 To decorate, spread a thin layer of sour cream on the top and dot with the fruit of your choice.

Fruit Fritters

For the Batter:

Imperial (Metric)	American
3 oz (85g) 85 per cent wheat flour	¾ cup 85 per cent wheat flour
1 oz (30g) gram (chick pea) flour	¼ cup gram (garbanzo bean) flour
Pinch sea salt	Pinch sea salt
1 tablespoon sunflower oil	1 tablespoon sunflower oil
¼ pint (140ml) water	⅔ cup water
1 egg white	1 egg white

Choice of fruit:

Imperial (Metric)	American
3 medium cooking apples, leave skins on, core and thinly slice	3 medium cooking apples, leave skins on, core and thinly slice
or	or
3 medium bananas, peel, cut lengthwise then cut in 3 making 18 pieces	3 medium bananas, peel, cut lengthwise then cut in 3 making 18 pieces
or	or
1 small pineapple, skinned, cut into rings and hard centres removed with a small cutter	1 small pineapple, skinned, cut into rings and hard centres removed with a small cutter
or	or
3 medium peaches, skinned by dropping in boiling water for ½ minute only. Cut in half, take out stones and slice in thin rings	3 medium peaches, skinned by dropping in boiling water for ½ minute only. Cut in half, take out stones and slice in thin rings
Soya oil for frying	Soy oil for frying

To make the batter:

1 Set *steel blades* in position. Sieve flours together, put into processor bowl with salt, oil and half the water. Blend until smooth. Then pour the remaining water through the feed tube and continue processing until well mixed.

2 Pour out into a mixing bowl. Wash and dry the processor bowl. Set *egg white whisk* in position. Whisk egg white until stiff.

3 Fold this into the batter with a metal spoon.

4 Leave to stand for 1 hour before using.

To make the fruit fritters:

1 Half fill your fryer with soya oil. Heat to approximately 370°F/190°C, which is moderately hot.

2 Stir batter and, using a skewer, dip fruit in. Allow excess batter to drip off and fry in hot oil for 2 to 3 minutes. Turn the fruit over after 1 minute. Cook only a few pieces at a time.

3 Drain on kitchen paper and keep warm in the oven on low heat, 300°F/150°C (Gas Mark 2), until all the fritters are done.

Note: You can serve these alone or dredged with a little fruit sugar which is white in colour and looks like castor sugar.

Almond Crêpes
Makes about 18

These are very light and especially delicious served with an apricot brandy sauce when entertaining or simply with a syrup made by sieving soft fruit and mixing with a little honey and water. Heat the sauce and pour over the crêpes just before serving.

For the almond crêpe batter:

Imperial (Metric)	American
3 oz (85g) wholemeal flour	¾ cup wholewheat flour
2 oz (55g) very finely ground almonds	½ cup very finely ground almonds
2 large eggs	2 large eggs
1 teaspoon fruit sugar	1 teaspoon fruit sugar
12 fl oz (340ml) milk	1½ cups milk
Good pinch sea salt	Good pinch sea salt
2 tablespoons sunflower oil	2 tablespoons sunflower oil
2 drops natural almond essence	2 drops natural almond essence
Little sunflower oil for frying	Little sunflower oil for frying

1 Set *steel blades* in position. Put flour, ground almonds, eggs, fruit sugar, half the milk, sea salt, sunflower oil and almond essence into the processor bowl. Blend well together. Gradually pour the remaining milk through the feed tube while motor is still running. Process until smooth. Let stand for 1 to 2 hours.

2 Stir batter before making the crêpes.

3 Heat the crêpe pan and, using a screwed-up piece of absorbent kitchen paper dipped in a little oil, wipe the surface of the hot pan.

4 When oil is almost smoking take off heat and put in 2 tablespoons of the batter. Tip and swirl the pan so that the batter spreads to the edges. Cook over medium heat for a minute, loosening the edges with a palette knife as it cooks.

5 When top has set, turn over and cook the other side. Watch carefully as this side will cook very quickly. It should be speckled light golden-brown.

Note: You can eat immediately for perfection, but they can be stacked one on top of the other until needed. They freeze well or can be stored in the fridge for 1 to 2 days wrapped in a clean dry cloth. If you leave out the fruit sugar and essence these can be savoury crêpes.

Apple and Date Stuffing for Almond Crêpes
To fill 10

Make up recipe for Almond Crêpes and then freeze those you have left over, ready for another stuffing. You might need more than 10 pancakes for this recipe — it depends on how generous you want to be with the filling.

Imperial (Metric)	American
Recipe for Almond Crêpes (see opposite)	Recipe for Almond Crêpes (see opposite)
1 oz (30g) polyunsaturated margarine	1 ounce polyunsaturated margarine
Juice and grated rind of ½ orange	Juice and grated rind of ½ orange
1 lb (455g) cooking apples, peeled, cored and chopped (weight with skins on)	1 pound cooking apples, peeled, cored and chopped (weight with skins on)
4 oz (115g) dates, chopped	⅔ cup chopped dates
¼ teaspoon clove powder	¼ teaspoon clove powder
½ teaspoon cinnamon	½ teaspoon cinnamon
1 to 2 tablespoons apple juice concentrate, to glaze	1 to 2 tablespoons apple juice concentrate, to glaze

1 Melt the margarine in a saucepan. Add the orange juice, rind, spices, apples and dates and cook gently for 10 minutes. Leave lid off and stir frequently.

2 Place a little filling on each pancake. Roll up and arrange in a greased ovenproof dish.

3 Pour a little apple juice concentrate over the top and heat in the oven, 325°F/160°C (Gas Mark 3), for 15 minutes.

Apricot and Almond Paste Pasties
Makes 12

For the pastry:

Imperial (Metric)	American
3 oz (85g) polyunsaturated margarine	⅓ cup polyunsaturated margarine
I level tablespoon fruit sugar	I level tablespoon fruit sugar
2 tablespoons natural yogurt	2 tablespoons plain yogurt
I egg yolk	I egg yolk
6 oz (170g) fine wholemeal flour	1½ cups fine wholewheat flour
Pinch sea salt	Pinch sea salt
½ teaspoon baking powder	½ teaspoon baking powder

For the filling:

Imperial (Metric)	American
1½ lbs (680g) ripe apricots	1½ pounds ripe apricots
4 oz (115g) fruit sugar	⅔ cup fruit sugar
I egg white	I egg white
I teaspoon lemon juice	I teaspoon lemon juice
2 drops natural almond essence	2 drops natural almond essence
4 oz (115g) finely ground almonds	I cup finely ground almonds

To make the pastry:

1 Set *steel blades* in position. Put margarine and sugar in the processor bowl. Cream together for ½ minute.

2 Add yogurt and egg yolk, plus 2 tablespoons of the flour, and salt and baking powder. Process until well mixed then gradually pour in the rest of the flour through the feed tube until all is mixed together, forming a soft but firm dough.

3 Put into a plastic bag and freeze for 15 minutes or refrigerate for 30 minutes to chill well.

4 Cut pastry in 12 equal parts. Roll each one into a ball and then on a floured surface roll each ball out thinly to a circle approximately 4 inches (10cm) in diameter. Now they are ready to fill.

For the filling:

1 Cut apricots in half to take out stones. Then slice each half thinly.

2 Set *steel blades* in position. Put sugar, egg white, lemon juice and essence into the processor bowl and blend well together. Gradually pour in the ground almonds, with the motor still on, until a paste is formed.

3 Dividing the fruit and paste equally, put slices of apricot in the centre of each pastry circle and dot flattened bits of almond paste over the top.

4 Egg brush the edges and fold over into a semi-circle shape, pressing wet edges together. Crimp edges, fork the top, egg-glaze the pastry and place on a greased baking tray.

5 Bake at 400°F/200°C (Gas Mark 6), for 10 minutes. Turn down to 350°F/180°C (Gas Mark 4) and continue baking for 10 to 15 minutes more until golden brown. While still hot sprinkle on a little fruit sugar if you like. Serve hot or cold.

Note: Alternatively you can make a pie using exactly the same ingredients. The pastry will line a 9 inch (23cm) pie dish and top the fruit when rolled out thinly. Bake the base blind for 10 minutes at 400°F/200°C (Gas Mark 6) centre shelf. Let cool. Fill with slices of apricot and dot with the paste. Top with thinly rolled out pastry. Egg glaze and bake at 400°F/200°C (Gas Mark 6) for 10 minutes, then 350°F/180°C (Gas Mark 4) for 20 more minutes.

Mince Pies
Makes 12

These are not just for Christmas, as the filling is less rich than the usual festive mincemeat. Make the mincemeat at least a day before needed, to allow a good flavour to develop. Jar the mincemeat and use when necessary.

For the mincemeat:

Imperial (Metric)	American
2 oz (55g) sunflower seeds	⅓ cup sunflower seeds
2 oz (55g) dates, steamed for 5 minutes only	⅓ cup dates, steamed for 5 minutes only
2 oz (55g) currants	⅓ cup currants
2 oz (55g) raisins	⅓ cup raisins
2 oz (55g) sultanas	⅓ cup golden seedless raisins
1 large cooking apple, cored and roughly chopped (leave skin on)	1 large cooking apple, cored and roughly chopped (leave skin on)
Juice and grated rind of ½ a lemon and ½ an orange	Juice and grated rind of ½ a lemon and ½ an orange
2 tablespoons apple juice concentrate	2 tablespoons apple juice concentrate
½ teaspoon freshly ground nutmeg	½ teaspoon freshly ground nutmeg
Pinch sea salt	Pinch sea salt
1 oz (28g) polyunsaturated margarine	2 tablespoons polyunsaturated margarine

1 Set *steel blades* in position and put sunflower seeds in the processor bowl. Chop for ½ minute.

2 Add all other ingredients and process until mushy.

3 Jar and use when needed. Will keep for two weeks in the fridge.

For the pastry:

You can use all wholemeal flour but I sometimes use three-quarters wholemeal and a quarter unbleached white flour for an extra light short pastry. Using baking powder lightens the dough even more, but is optional because even small amounts kill some of the vitamin B in wholemeal flour, so always use sparingly.

Imperial (Metric)	American
6 oz (170g) wholemeal flour	1½ cups wholewheat flour
2 oz (55g) unbleached white flour	½ cup unbleached white flour
1 very level teaspoon baking powder (optional)	1 very level teaspoon baking powder (optional)
1 dessertspoon fruit sugar	2 teaspoons fruit sugar
4 oz (115g) polyunsaturated margarine	½ cup polyunsaturated margarine
1 egg yolk	1 egg yolk
2 tablespoons cold water	2 tablespoons cold water

1 Sieve flours and baking powder together in a mixing bowl.

2 Set *steel blades* in position. Put sugar and margarine into the processor bowl and cream together until well blended.

3 Hand whisk egg yolk with the water until frothy and pour into the creamed mixture, along with 2 tablespoons of the flours, through the feed tube while motor is running.

4 Gradually add the rest of the flour mixture. Leave motor on for 30 seconds after the ingredients have blended well together.

5 Scoop out and put the dough into a plastic bag and freeze for 10 minutes or refrigerate for 30 minutes before rolling out.

To make the mince pies:

1 Grease the bun tin and roll out pastry quite thinly on a floured surface. To avoid using too much flour or the rolling pin sticking, place a sheet of polythene over the pastry and roll out. Use a medium and small cutter.

2 Place 12 medium size pastry rounds into the bun tin and spoon in the mincemeat mixture.

3 Eggwash the edge of the underside of the smaller rounds of pastry. Pop them on top of the filling. They should just cover the edge of the bottom pastry rounds. Fork the top, brush with egg and sprinkle on a little fruit sugar (optional). Bake at 375°F/190°C (Gas Mark 5) for 20 to 25 minutes maximum.

Note: You can make one large 8 inch (20cm) pie with the ingredients, but bake at 400°F/200°C (Gas Mark 6) for 10 minutes, turning down heat to 350°F/180°C (Gas Mark 4) for a further 20 minutes.

Sweet Rice Balls

Rice is rarely used in the West as a sweet except for white rice pudding, which is unfortunate because it makes a lovely light but satisfying dessert mixed with dried or fresh fruits. Here is my favourite, but experiment further and you will be surprised how delicious sweet rice balls can be. Cook rice a day before or use left-overs.

Imperial (Metric)	American
8 oz (225g) short grain Italian brown rice	I cup short grain Italian brown rice
½ teaspoon sea salt	½ teaspoon sea salt
4 oz (115g) raisins	⅔ cup raisins
2 tablespoons lemon juice plus grated rind of I lemon	2 tablespoons lemon juice plus grated rind of I lemon
2 level tablespoons honey	2 level tablespoons honey
2 pieces of stem ginger, chopped into small bits	2 pieces of stem ginger, chopped into small bits
2 oz (55g) dried apricots	⅓ cup dried apricots
4 oz (115g) almonds	I cup almonds

1 Measure out rice by cupfuls. Wash well in a sieve. To each cup of rice add 2 cups water.

2 Bring rice and water, plus the sea salt, to boil. Turn down to simmer. Cover tightly and cook for 35 minutes on low heat.

3 Leave lid on after cooking. This will soften the rice and make it more glutinous. Stand for 10 minutes.

4 Set *steel blades* in position. Put rice into the bowl and process briefly. This breaks the rice grains up a little and helps when making the rice balls. Take out and leave overnight, covered.

5 Soak raisins in the lemon juice, rind, ginger and honey overnight.

6 Soak apricots in hot water overnight. Drain.

7 Chop apricots and stir into the rice with the raisin mixture.

8 Set *steel blades* in position and chop almonds until medium ground, but not powdery.

9 Toast under a grill, using moderate heat, until lightly browned.

10 Form rice mixture into 10 balls and roll in the toasted almonds. Chill.

Variation:
Try toasted sesame seeds to coat and other soaked dried fruit such as chopped figs or dates, or add chopped nuts or sunflower seeds to the mixture to vary the flavour of this wholesome dessert.

5.

BREAD, CAKES AND BISCUITS

Your processor is invaluable in helping to take the chore out of making tea-time treats. Not everyone likes wallowing in flour and yeasty liquids or laboriously kneading or creaming mixtures as much as I do. If I was not a cook, I'm sure I would be a potter, because of my love of making bread. I am amazed at how many of my students have an aversion to touching doughs of any kind. So, for those of you who feel this way, your processor will perhaps encourage you to do more home baking.

With the wonderful, wholesome variety of ingredients available, your efforts will be well rewarded. Not only can the treats be enjoyed but they can also be jam-packed with goodness. For a start, using wheatmeal, cornmeal, rye and soya flour, a few sesame seeds, a little malt extract and caraway seeds, you can turn the ordinary loaf, our 'staff of life', into a mouth-watering experience. Using nuts, seeds, dried and fresh fruit and, of course, wholemeal flour your cakes and biscuits will nourish as well as satisfy.

To stimulate the taste buds with a reasonably clear conscience is a double pleasure. Yes, we do have to eat less sugar and saturated fats (see page 10 for more information), but eating moderately, choosing natural ingredients without additives, synthetic colourings and flavourings and — I can't state this often enough — by cutting down on our intake of those foods which are detrimental to our health, I think we can cope with a few indulgences. So here goes with some of earth's bountiful goodness to help you create gorgeous goodies for all to enjoy.

Bread and Other Yeasted Doughs

It is most important that you do not overload your processor. Stick to the amounts given in the recipes and you can't go wrong. If I want to make a large batch of bread I mix all the ingredients well together in a mixing bowl then knead it bit by bit in the processor for one minute only. For example, if you are using a 3.3 pound (1.5 kilo) bag of flour, which will make you five 1 pound (455g) loaves, then break the dough into five equal parts and process each piece separately. It will take five minutes and save your wrist muscles.

The recipes I give are for small amounts but just double or treble etc., the ingredients as you wish. An important point to remember is that you do not need to increase the yeast as much as the other ingredients. For example, say your machine will take a dough which has 12-14 ounces (340-395g) flour using ½ ounce (15g) dried yeast or 1 ounce (28g) fresh yeast. If you use 3.3 pounds (1.5 kilo) of flour you will only need 1 ounce (28g) dried yeast or 2 ounces (55g) fresh yeast. Throughout the mixing and rising the yeast works best when kept warm. If it is too hot it will die and if too cold the yeast grows too slowly and your bread will be like lead.

Using a strong flour which has a higher content of gluten will result in a good-textured loaf. Gluten is the protein in wheat and has a stretchy, rubbery quality. It forms little tiny balloons which are filled with the carbon dioxide which is made when the yeast, feeding on natural sugars in the dough, multiplies. A draught can flatten these bubbles and make the resulting bread heavy. So keep your dough in a warm, protected place when rising.

Basic Wholemeal Loaf with Sesame Seeds

Preheat oven to 450°F/230°C (Gas Mark 8) 20 minutes before you are ready to bake. This recipe will fit a 1 pound (445g) loaf tin.

Imperial (Metric)	American
8 fl oz (200ml) warm water	1 cup warm water
½ oz (15g) dried yeast *or* 1 oz (28g) fresh	½ ounce dried yeast *or* 1 ounce fresh
½ teaspoon Barbados sugar	½ teaspoon Barbados sugar
1 tablespoon sesame seeds, lightly toasted	1 tablespoon sesame seeds, lightly toasted
12 oz (340g) strong wholemeal flour	3 cups strong wholewheat flour
1 level teaspoon sea salt	1 level teaspoon sea salt
1 generous teaspoon malt extract	1 generous teaspoon malt syrup
1 dessertspoon sunflower oil	2 teaspoons sunflower oil

1 Sprinkle dried yeast into the warm water. Stir in the sugar and leave to froth in a warm place for approximately 10 minutes. If using fresh yeast, cream the sugar and yeast then gradually add the warm water.

2 Toast the sesame seeds in a heavy-bottomed dry pan on moderate heat until lightly browned and popping.

3 Set *steel blades* in position. Put flour, sea salt and sesame seeds into the bowl.

4 When yeast liquid is frothy stir in the malt extract (syrup) and oil. With motor running, pour the liquid down the feed tube. Continue processing until the mixture forms into a smooth and elastic dough, which takes approximately 60 seconds.

5 Place dough in a greased polythene bag. Press out the air and secure the opening. Wrap in a warm towel and leave to rise in a warm place for 40 minutes or until doubled in size.

6 Return the risen dough to the processor and re-knead for abut 10 seconds. With floured hands knead the dough for 30 seconds. Shape into the greased and lightly-floured tin. Press dough into the corners gently with your fist.

7 Put into the greased plastic bag and leave to rise in a warm place until the dough has risen to the top of the tin.

8 Bake at 450°F/230°C (Gas Mark 8) for 10 minutes. Turn down heat to 375°F/190°C (Gas Mark 5) for 20 to 25 minutes. Loosen edges with a palette knife. Cool on a wire rack.

Granary French Loaf
Makes two 10 inch/25 cm loaves

Preheat oven to 425°F/220°C (Gas Mark 7) 20 minutes before you are ready to bake.

Imperial (Metric)	American
½ oz (15g) dried yeast	½ ounce dried yeast
7 fl oz (175ml) warm water	¾ cup warm water
1 level teaspoon Barbados sugar	1 level teaspoon Barbados sugar
12 oz (170g) granary flour	3 cups granary flour
1 very level teaspoon sea salt	1 very level teaspoon sea salt
1 level dessertspoon malt extract	2 level teaspoons malt syrup
3 teaspoons sunflower oil	3 teaspoons sunflower oil
A little cracked wheat for top	A little cracked wheat for top

1 Sprinkle dried yeast on the warm water. Stir in the sugar and leave to froth in a warm place for approximately 10 minutes.

2 Set *steel blades* in position. Put flour and sea salt in the bowl.

3 When yeast liquid is frothy stir in the malt extract (syrup) and oil. While motor is running pour the liquid down the feed tube. Continue processing until the mixture forms into a smooth and elastic dough. (Takes approximately 60 seconds.)

4 Place dough in a greased polythene bag. Press out the air and secure the opening. Wrap in a warm towel and leave to rise in a warm place for 1 hour or until double in size.

5 Return the risen dough to the processor bowl, re-knead for about 10 seconds.

6 Take out dough and with floured hands knead it for 30 seconds. Halve the dough and put one half back in the bag.

7 On a lightly-floured surface, roll out remaining dough to a long thickish oval shape. Then roll up as you would a Swiss-roll, pressing the dough gently to form a 10 inch (25cm) French loaf shape. Place on a greased and floured baking tray.

8 Repeat with the other half. You should get both on the one tray.

9 Slide tray into a large polythene bag and leave to rise in a warm place for about 30 minutes or until double in size.

10 With a knife, make four to five diagonal slits in each loaf. Brush the top with a little warm water and sprinkle with cracked wheat.

11 Bake in the centre of the oven for 20 minutes, until the bread sounds hollow when you tap the underside. Cool on a wire rack.

Note: You can shape the dough into a round but, as it will be denser, it will need more time to bake: 20 minutes on 425°F/220°C (Gas Mark 7) and 15 minutes on 375°F/190°C (Gas Mark 5).

Rye Bread with Orange and Caraway

To make truly delicious chewy and not too heavy bread you have to use a combination of wheat and rye flour. You can buy dark or light rye flour. The darker variety has much more flavour but does not rise so easily and the bread is heavier. You can use either dark or light rye flour with this recipe. The rising time is long because of the smaller amount of gluten in rye flour. Set oven to 425°F/220°C (Gas Mark 7) 20 minutes before you bake.

Imperial (Metric)	American
½ oz (15g) dried yeast *or* I oz (30g) fresh yeast	½ ounce dried yeast *or* I ounce fresh yeast
9 fl oz warm water	1¼ cups warm water
2½ teaspoons molasses	2½ teaspoons molasses
6 oz (170g) rye flour	1½ cups rye flour
8 oz (225g) wholemeal flour	2 cups wholewheat flour
I level teaspoon sea salt	I level teaspoon sea salt
I tablespoon sunflower oil	I tablespoon sunflower oil
Grated rind of I orange	Grated rind of I orange
I level teaspoon caraway seeds	I level teaspoon caraway seeds
A little milk to brush top	A little milk to brush top
A few caraway seeds to sprinkle on top	A few caraway seeds to sprinkle on top

1 Sprinkle yeast on the warm water. Stir in ½ teaspoon molasses and leave to rise in a warm place for 10 minutes.

2 Set *steel blades* in position and put flours and sea salt into the bowl.

3 When yeast liquid is frothy, stir in the rest of the molasses, the oil, the orange rind and the caraway seeds.

4 Switch on the processor and pour in the liquid. Leave on until a smooth dough is formed, approximately 60 seconds.

5 With floured hands take out dough and mould for 30 seconds.

6 Put into a greased polythene bag and leave to rise in a warm place for 1½ to 2 hours.

7 Knead dough for 10 seconds more.

8 With floured hands, form dough into an oval shape. Place on a greased baking tray and prick the top all over with a fork.

9 Slide into the greased polythene bag and leave to rise for a further 1½ hours until doubled in size.

10 Brush the top with milk and a sprinkling of caraway seeds.

11 Bake in the centre of the oven at 425°F/220°C (Gas Mark 7) for 15 minutes. Lower the heat to 375°F/190°C (Gas Mark 5) and continue to bake for a further 35 minutes. Your loaf will be baked when it sounds hollow when tapped underneath. Cool on a wire rack.

High Protein Loaf
To fit a 1 pound (455g) loaf tin

Preheat oven to 450°F/230°C (Gas Mark 8) 20 minutes before you bake.

Imperial (Metric)	American
2 oz (55g) sunflower seeds *or* sprouted wheat (see page 112 on sprouting your own seeds)	⅓ cup sunflower seeds *or* sprouted wheat (see page 112 on sprouting your own seeds)
½ oz (15g) dried yeast *or* 1 oz (30g) fresh yeast	½ ounce dried yeast *or* 1 ounce fresh yeast
½ pint (285ml) warm water	1⅓ cups warm water
½ teaspoon Barbados sugar	½ teaspoon Barbados sugar
10 oz (285g) wholemeal flour	2½ cups wholewheat flour
1 oz (28g) soya flour	¼ cup soy flour
2 rounded tablespoons wheatgerm	2 rounded tablespoons wheatgerm
2 level tablespoons fine oatmeal	2 level tablespoons fine oatmeal
1 teaspoon sea salt	1 teaspoon sea salt
1 dessertspoon dried skimmed milk powder	2 teaspoons dried skimmed milk powder
1 dessertspoon malt extract *or* molasses	2 teaspoons malt syrup *or* molasses
1 tablespoon sunflower oil	1 tablespoon sunflower oil

1 If using sunflower seeds toast in a dry pan on moderate heat, stirring constantly until lightly browned.

2 Sprinkle yeast onto half the warm water. Stir in the sugar and leave to froth in a warm place.

3 Set *steel blades* in position and roughly grind the toasted sunflower seeds.

4 Add wholemeal flour, soya flour, wheatgerm, fine oatmeal and sea salt.

5 When yeast liquid has frothed, mix with the rest of the water, milk powder, malt extract (syrup) or molasses and the oil and, with motor running, pour the liquid down the feed tube. Continue processing until the mixture forms into a smooth dough. (Takes approximately 60 seconds.)

6 Put dough into a greased polythene bag. Press out the air and secure the top. Wrap in a warm towel. Let rise in a warm place for about 1 hour or until double in size.

7 Return to the processor, re-knead for about 10 seconds.

8 Turn onto a lightly floured surface. Form into a loaf shape and press this into the greased and floured tin, making sure the dough touches the edges and corners of the tin.

9 Slide into a greased polythene bag and let rise for approximately 40 minutes or until doubled in size. Bake at 450°F/230°C (Gas Mark 8) for 10 minutes. Turn down heat to 375°F/190°C (Gas Mark 5) for 20 minutes to 25 minutes. Cool on a wire rack.

Wholemeal Pitta Bread

The first time I ate pitta bread was in Greece many years ago. It was stuffed with crisp lettuce and a delightful tasting purée called Hummous (page 33 for recipe). As I couldn't find a recipe then I experimented. At first the pittas were too thick and I couldn't get them to separate in the middle. With a bit of trial and error I finally produced perfect pittas. The secret is to roll them out thinly and bake them in a very hot oven for only 5 minutes.

Follow the recipe for Basic Wholemeal Loaf with Sesame Seeds (page 156). The dough will yield you 8 pittas. When dough has risen to double its size, and with *steel blades* in position, process for 10 seconds. Set the oven to 450°F/230°C (Gas Mark 8) 20 minutes before you bake the first batch.

1 Break dough into 8 equal parts. Roll out one at a time, keeping the unused dough in the polythene bag.

2 Roll each piece in bran, not flour, to an oval shape approximately 8 inches (20cm) long and 4 inches (10cm) wide.

3 Place each oval onto warmed trays which you have sprinkled with bran.

4 Slide trays into greased polythene bags as you fill them.

5 Leave to rise slightly in a warm place for approximately 20 minutes.

6 Bake each tray separately on the top shelf of the oven. Cool on a wire rack.

Note: They will either puff up completely or in parts; either way they will open easily to stuff. When cold, flatten slightly and freeze any that are not needed. To defrost put in a moderate oven for 2 minutes only.

Fillings for Pitta Bread

Your pittas will make a truly wholesome, well-balanced, light but satisfying meal if you choose the right fillings. I will give three ideas which I hope will delight your palate and will certainly nourish your body.

Filling 1 Serves 4:

This is the simplest filling of all since most of it is a ready supply of Cheddar cheese. I choose bean sprouts to boost the protein as well as giving that fresh crunchy texture. This is really deluxe Welsh Rarebit.

Imperial (Metric)	American
4 pitta breads	4 pitta breads
A little polyunsaturated margarine	A little polyunsaturated margarine
6 oz (170g) Cheddar cheese	1½ cups Cheddar cheese
Sprinkling of cayenne pepper (optional)	Sprinkling of cayenne pepper (optional)
4 spring onions, chopped finely	4 scallions, chopped finely
5 oz (140g) bean sprouts	2 cups bean sprouts
1 medium red pepper	1 medium red pepper
A little shoyu (naturally fermented soya sauce)	A little naturally fermented soy sauce

1 Cut each pitta open so that you have two ovals.

2 Spread halves with a little polyunsaturated margarine.

3 With *shredding plate* in position cut cheese to a size to fit feed tube. Using pusher, press cheese firmly down, grate.

4 Sprinkle grated cheese on one half of each pitta and grill until lightly brown. If using cayenne pepper use just a small pinch to top cheese.

5 Mix chopped spring onions (scallions) with the bean sprouts and sprinkle over the cheese.

6 With a sharp knife cut a circle around the stalk end of the red pepper. Take out core and seeds, then slice in half lengthwise to fit feed tube. Stand each half upright in feed tube and slice.

7 Spread thin slices of red pepper over the bean sprouts.

8 Shake a little shoyu (soy sauce) over the top. Cap with the other half of the pitta bread and put under grill for 30 seconds only. Serve hot.

Filling II *Serves 4:*

Imperial (Metric)	American
4 pitta breads	4 pitta breads
A little polyunsaturated margarine	A little polyunsaturated margarine
8 oz (225g) Hummous (see page 33 for recipe)	1⅓ cups Hummous (see page 33 for recipe)
½ crisp lettuce	½ crisp lettuce

1 Warm pitta breads in the oven for 1 to 2 minutes only.

2 Slice in half widthwise so that you have two pockets.

3 Open, spread a little margarine inside each pocket.

4 Wash and towel-dry the lettuce and line the pitta pockets with whole lettuce leaves.

5 Stuff one heaped tablespoon hummous in the centre of the lettuce and serve.

Filling III *Serves 4:*

Imperial (Metric)	American
4 pitta breads	4 pitta breads
A little polyunsaturated margarine	A little polyunsaturated margarine
8 oz (225g) Spicy Lentil and Mushroom Pâté (see page 28 for recipe)	1⅓ cups Spicy Lentil and Mushroom Pâté (see page 28 for recipe)
10 thin slices of tomato	10 thin slices of tomato
8 thin rings onion	8 thin rings onion

1 Warm the pittas and slice open so that you have two ovals.

2 Spread both halves with margarine and on one half put two tablespoons of the spicy lentil mixture.

3 Top with two onion rings and four slices of tomato to each portion.

4 Cap with the other half of pitta and serve.

Wholemeal Pizza
Makes one 12 inch (30cm) pizza

Pizza can so often be an abomination comprising a tasteless 'cardboard' base topped with a dollop of tomato purée, meagre scraps and a bit of grated cheese. This recipe is richly endowed with all the goodness and flavour of a real Italian pizza. You can use the Basic Wholemeal Loaf with Sesame Seeds (see page 156) for the base or in fact any good bread dough will do. When making batches of bread I usually put aside approximately 12 ounces (340g) of dough which is the amount you would need to fit a 12 inch (30cm) pizza tray. But I have given another dough with just that extra richness a pizza should have. I choose pumpkin seeds instead of olives to garnish when making pizza for children.

Imperial (Metric)	American
2½ fl oz (75ml) milk	Just under ⅓ cup milk
⅓ oz dried or ¾ oz fresh yeast	⅓ ounce dried or ¾ ounce fresh yeast
I very level teaspoon Barbados sugar	I very level teaspoon Barbados sugar
8 oz (225g) wholemeal flour	2 cups wholewheat flour
I very level teaspoon sea salt	I very level teaspoon sea salt
2 tablespoons olive oil	2 tablespoons olive oil
I large egg, beaten	I large egg, beaten
Bran for rolling out dough	Bran for rolling out dough
½ quantity Pizza Sauce (see page 125)	½ quantity Pizza Sauce (see page 125)
6 oz (170g) Mozzarella, thinly sliced or grated farmhouse Cheddar cheese	⅔ cup Mozzarella, thinly sliced or grated farmhouse Cheddar cheese
3 oz (85g) stoned black olives or 2 oz (55g) pumpkin seeds	¾ cup stoned black olives or ½ cup pumpkin seeds
½ teaspoon basil to garnish	½ teaspoon basil to garnish

1 Warm the milk until tepid. If using dried yeast sprinkle it into the milk with sugar. Stir well until dissolved. If using fresh yeast just cream with the sugar and a few drops of tepid milk. Stir in rest of milk.

2 With *steel blades* in position put flour and salt into the bowl. With the motor running pour in yeast liquid, oil and beaten egg. Continue to process until a smooth dough is formed. (Takes approximately 60 seconds.)

3 With your hands shape dough into a ball and place in an oiled polythene bag. Leave to rise in a warm place until double in size, about an hour.

4 Make sauce now and leave aside to cool slightly.

5 When the dough has risen return to processor and re-knead for 10 seconds.

6 Sprinkle bran onto a clean work surface and roll out the dough from a ball shape to a circle 12 inches (30cm) across.

7 Place on your oiled pizza tray. Cover with a damp cloth and let rise for just 15 minutes in a warm place.

8 Ladle on the sauce to within 1 inch (2.5cm) of the outer edge. (If sauce has too much liquid remove some and use it in a gravy or soup.)

9 Place slices of cheese, slightly overlapping, on top or sprinkle on the Cheddar. Dot with olives or pumpkin seeds and finally sprinkle on the basil.

10 Bake at 425°F/220°C (Gas Mark 7) near the top of the oven for 20 to 25 minutes, or until cheese is golden-brown and the base well risen. Let stand 10 minutes before cutting. Serve with a fresh, green, dressed salad.

Wholemeal Scones
Makes about 8

I use pastry flour for this recipe as it has a low gluten content which is desirable when using baking powder to make scones or quick breads. Do not process too long.

Imperial (Metric)	American
8 oz (225g) wholemeal pastry flour	2 cups wholewheat pastry flour
1 rounded teaspoon baking powder	1 rounded teaspoon baking soda
1 dessertspoon Barbados sugar (optional)	2 teaspoons Barbados sugar (optional)
½ teaspoon sea salt	½ teaspoon sea salt
1½ oz (45g) polyunsaturated margarine	3 tablespoons polyunsaturated margarine
5 fl oz (140ml) natural yogurt	⅔ cup plain yogurt

1 Heat oven to 425°F/220°C (Gas Mark 7).

2 With *steel blades* in position, put flour, baking powder, sugar (if used), salt and margarine in the bowl and process until blended.

3 Add yogurt and continue to process until mixture forms into a ball of dough — about 10 seconds only.

4 Roll out on a floured board to about ¾ inch (2cm) thickness and cut into 2½ inch (6cm) rounds.

5 Place on an oiled and lightly floured baking tray. Brush the tops with milk and bake for 12 to 15 minutes.

Variations:
Fruit Scones: Add 3 oz (85g/½ cup) sultanas (golden seedless raisins) just before adding the yogurt.

Cheese Scones: I use 81 per cent extraction flour, omit the sugar and add 4 oz (115g/1 cup) grated farmhouse Cheddar. Add the cheese just before the yogurt.

Oat Scones: Substitute 2 oz (55g/½ cup) fine oatmeal for 2 oz (55g/½ cup) of the wholemeal flour.

Cornmeal Scones: Substitute 4 oz (115g/1 cup) cornmeal for 4 oz (115g/1 cup) wholemeal flour.

Wheatmeal Scones: Use half wheatmeal flour and half unbleached white flour.

Cakes

Your processor will help you to make a enormous variety of cakes and biscuits. I will endeavour to make them as healthy as possible, a difficult task when using sugar and any concentrated sweeteners.

In sweet baking I try to use wholemeal flour, plus other fibrous and nutritious foods such as nuts, seeds and dried and fresh fruit, as much as possible. This is most important when sugar is amongst the ingredients. We need the fibre to offset the adverse effects of certain foods, sugar being top of the list. See notes on fibre and sugar, pages 9 and 11.

I have chosen a few unusual recipes for your sweet bakes which might seem a bit different from the regular cookbook variety, but I think you will be pleasantly surprised at their taste and texture.

Apricot and Cardamom Cake

Mixture will fit an 8 inch (20cm) cake tin, greased and lined. Set oven to 325°F/160°C (Gas Mark 3).

Imperial (Metric)	American
4 oz (115g) dried apricots	¾ cup dried apricots
6 oz (170g) clear honey	½ cup clear honey
Seeds from 4 cardamoms, crushed	Seeds from 4 cardamoms, crushed
6 oz (170g) polyunsaturated margarine	¾ cup polyunsaturated margarine
3 eggs, beaten	3 eggs, beaten
8 oz (225g) self-raising wholemeal flour, sifted	2 cups self-raising wholewheat flour, sifted

1 Soak apricots in boiling water for half an hour, just to soften. Drain and dry on absorbent kitchen paper. Chop roughly by hand.

2 Set *steel blades* in position. Put in honey, crushed cardamom seeds and margarine. Process for 30 seconds. Gradually add the beaten eggs.

3 Add the sifted flour a tablespoon at a time using the *pulse*. When completely blended take off lid of bowl.

4 Sprinkle the chopped apricots over the mixture evenly, replace the lid and, using pulse button, incorporate the fruit.

5 Spoon into the lined cake tin and bake for 1 hour.

American Festive Cake

This is a rich fruity cake with those delicious pecan nuts which have the texture of walnuts but are not bitter. The size is exactly half my usual family Christmas cake and is just right for a Christmas gift for someone who perhaps lives alone, or an elderly couple. Lots of goodies are cooked at Christmas time simply because we have family or friends to feed, so spare a thought for those who are less fortunate.

The mixture will fit a 7 inch (18cm) cake tin, greased and lined. Preheat oven to 300°F/150°C (Gas Mark 2).

Imperial (Metric)	American
4 oz (115g) polyunsaturated margarine, chilled	½ cup polyunsaturated margarine, chilled
3 oz (85g) Barbados sugar	½ cup Barbados sugar
2 large eggs, beaten	2 large eggs, beaten
6 oz (170g) wholemeal flour	1½ cups wholewheat flour
1 level teaspoon freshly grated nutmeg } sieved together	1 level teaspoon freshly grated nutmeg } sieved together
¼ teaspoon clove powder	¼ teaspoon clove powder
Juice and rind of ½ orange	Juice and rind of ½ orange
Juice and rind of ½ lemon	Juice and rind of ½ lemon
3 fl oz (120ml) brandy	⅓ cup brandy
3 oz (85g) each raisins, sultanas and currants	½ cup each dark and golden seedless raisins and currants
2 oz (55g) dried apricots, chopped	⅓ cup dried apricots, chopped
1½ oz (45g) each crystallized cherries and pineapple	¼ cup each crystallized cherries and pineapple
1 oz (30g) dried apple flakes *or* dried apple rings, chopped	½ cup dried apple flakes *or* dried apple rings, chopped
2 oz (55g) pecan nuts, roughly chopped by hand	½ cup pecan nuts, roughly chopped by hand
1 oz (30g) pecan nuts *and* 1 oz (30g) glacé cherries, to decorate	¼ cup pecan nuts *and* ¼ cup glacé cherries, to decorate

1 With *steel blades* in position, spoon the chilled margarine into the processor bowl.

2 Add sugar and mix for 45 seconds, scraping down the bowl several times.

3 Add the eggs through feed tube, a tablespoon at a time, with motor on.

4 Remove lid of bowl and sprinkle the flour all around the egg mixture. Replace lid and *pulse* only until the ingredients are all incorporated. Gently pulse in juice of orange and lemon, together with 2 tablespoons brandy.

5 Add orange and lemon rind, fruit and nuts and mix again using *pulse* button (using normal speed would chop the fruit too finely).

6 Scoop out mixture, giving it a gentle stir and turn into the prepared tin.

7 Decorate the top with glacé cherries and pecans.

8 Bake for 2 hours. While cake is still hot spoon over the remaining brandy.

Apple and Date Cake

This cake will fit a 7 inch (18cm) cake tin or a 1 pound (455g) loaf tin. Preheat the oven to 350°F/180°C (Gas Mark 4).

Imperial (Metric)	American
4 oz (115g) polyunsaturated margarine	½ cup polyunsaturated margarine
3oz (85g) Barbados sugar	½ cup Barbados sugar
2 eggs, beaten	2 eggs, beaten
6 oz (170g) self-raising wholemeal flour ⎫	1½ cups self-raising wholewheat flour ⎫
¼ teaspoon clove powder ⎬ sieved together	¼ teaspoon clove powder ⎬ sieved together
½ teaspoon ground cinnamon ⎭	½ teaspoon ground cinnamon ⎭
8 oz (225g) cooking apples, cored and chopped but not peeled	8 ounces cooking apples, cored and chopped but not peeled
2 oz (55g) chopped dates	⅓ cup chopped dates

1 Set *steel blades* in position. Put margarine and sugar in the bowl. Mix together for 45 seconds. You will have to stop the motor several times to scrape down the bowl. Mixture should be light and fluffy.

2 With motor on, add beaten eggs a tablespoon at a time.

3 Add the sieved flour and spices a tablespoon at a time using *pulse* to blend each tablespoonful in. Stop machine.

4 Remove lid of bowl and sprinkle on the fruit and again use pulse until incorporated.

5 Scoop into the greased and lined tin and bake in the centre of the oven for 1 hour. Test with a sharp knife. If it's not sticky your cake is done.

Carob Birthday Cake

Children's birthday parties can be great fun, even with a few scuffles. They can also be a reasonably healthy event when not overloaded with pink icing. So here goes with a wholesome birthday cake using carob powder to give a chocolate-like flavour. Carob is caffeine-free, naturally sweet and much cheaper than chocolate. Another reason for using this product instead of chocolate is that the cocoa bean is high in oxalic acid, which is known to 'lock in' calcium and thus make it unavailable to the body.

The mixture will need two 8½ inch (21cm) loose-bottomed cake tins, greased and lined. Measure the ingredients out in two batches so you do not overload the processor. Set oven to 350°F/180°C (Gas Mark 4).

Imperial (Metric)	American
8 oz (225g) polyunsaturated margarine	I cup polyunsaturated margarine
6 oz (170g) fruit sugar	I cup fruit sugar
4 eggs, beaten	4 eggs, beaten
2 level tablespoons finely ground almonds	2 level tablespoons finely ground almonds
8 oz (225g) self-raising wholemeal pastry flour minus 4 level tablespoons } sieved together	2 cups self-raising wholewheat pastry flour minus 4 level tablespoons } sieved together
2 level tablespoons carob powder	2 level tablespoons carob powder
4 drops natural vanilla essence	4 drops natural vanilla essence

1 Divide ingredients and process exactly half at a time.

2 With *steel blades* in position put margarine and sugar in the bowl. Cream together for 45 seconds. Stop motor to scrape down sides whilst creaming.

3 *Pulse* 10 times then, with motor on, spoon beaten eggs, in a tablespoon at a time, through feed tube. Switch motor off.

4 Stir ground almonds into the sifted flour and carob mixture.

5 Drop vanilla essence through feed tube and, with motor running, spoon in the dry ingredients until just blended.

6 Scoop into the lined tin and bake for 30 to 35 minutes on middle shelf. Repeat with second half of ingredients. Cool on a wire rack and decorate when cold.

For the topping:

Imperial (Metric)	American
2 level tablespoons polyunsaturated margarine	2 level tablespoons polyunsaturated margarine
2 oz (55g) dried skimmed milk powder	½ cup dried skimmed milk powder
1 level tablespoon carob powder	1 level tablespoon carob powder
2 tablespoons clear honey	2 tablespoons clear honey
4 oz (115g) yogurt cheese* or double cream	½ cup yogurt cheese* or heavy cream
A few drops natural vanilla essence	A few drops natural vanilla essence
2 tablespoons no-sugar berry jam	2 tablespoons no-sugar berry jam

1 Set *steel blades* in position and process margarine and milk powder.

2 Add carob and blend using *pulse*.

3 Add honey, yogurt cheese or cream and vanilla essence, and mix together, using *pulse*.

4 When cake is cold spread the jam on the two undersides of the cake. Spread a thickish layer of the topping on one layer and top with other layer.

5 Spread the remaining jam on the top of the cake and cover with the cream topping.

*To make yogurt cheese just drip ½ pint (285ml/1⅓ cups) natural yogurt through a muslin overnight or for a few hours.

Beetroot (Beet) and Walnut Cake

You might be surprised to see beetroot (beet) as an ingredient in a cake but, combined with certain ingredients, it is quite delicious.

Set oven to 325°F/160°C (Gas Mark 3). The mixture will fit a 7 inch (18cm) round or 1 pound (455g) loaf tin.

Imperial (Metric)	American
4 oz (115g) thinly peeled raw beetroot	½ cup thinly peeled raw beet
4 oz (115g) washed and scraped raw carrot	4 ounces washed and scraped raw carrot
2 oz (55g) walnuts	½ cup English walnuts
6 fl oz (180ml) corn or sunflower oil	¾ cup corn or sunflower oil
3 oz (85g) Barbados sugar	½ cup Barbados sugar
2 eggs, beaten	2 eggs, beaten
6 oz (170g) wholemeal flour ⎫	1½ cups wholewheat flour ⎫
¼ teaspoon ground clove powder ⎬ sieved	¼ teaspoon ground clove powder ⎬ sieved
1 teaspoon cinnamon ⎭ together	1 teaspoon cinnamon ⎭ together

1 Set *shredding plate* in position. Cut off pieces of beetroot to fit feed tube almost to the top, and push firmly down with the pusher.

2 Repeat with carrots and mix both together. Clean out processor bowl.

3 With *steel blades* in position chop nuts roughly for a few seconds. Scoop out and leave aside.

4 Still with steel blades in position put oil and sugar in the bowl. Process for 15 seconds.

5 Add beaten eggs gradually through feed tube.

6 Add flour and spices a tablespoon at a time, using *pulse* to merge each tablespoon in. Stop machine. Take off lid of processor bowl.

7 Sprinkle the grated beetroot (beet), carrots and nuts over the top of the mixture. Replace lid.

8 Using *pulse* incorporate the vegetables into the mixture.

9 Scoop into the greased and lined tin and bake for 1 hour. Test with a sharp knife. If not sticky then the cake is cooked.

Variation:
Carrot and Hazelnut Cake: Follow recipe for Beetroot and Walnut Cake but use 8 oz (225g) grated carrot and no beetroot, hazelnuts instead of walnuts and leave out the cinnamon.

Biscuits

Coconut and Lemon Cookies
Makes approx. 4 dozen

Imperial (Metric)	American
6 oz (170g) polyunsaturated margarine	¾ cup polyunsaturated margarine
4½ oz (130g) Demerara sugar	¾ cup Demerara sugar
2 eggs, beaten	2 eggs, beaten
8 oz (225g) wholemeal pastry flour, sifted	2 cups wholewheat pastry flour, sifted
2 tablespoons lemon juice	2 tablespoons lemon juice
Grated rind of 1 lemon	Grated rind of 1 lemon
A few drops natural vanilla essence	A few drops natural vanilla essence
1½ oz (45g) desiccated coconut	½ cup desiccated coconut

1 Preheat oven to 350°F/180°C (Gas Mark 4).

2 Set *steel blades* in position. Mix margarine and sugar for 45 seconds. Scrape down bowl as needed.

3 Pour eggs through feed tube and beat in.

4 Take off lid and sprinkle on the flour. Using *pulse*, blend together.

5 Add lemon juice, rind, vanilla essence and coconut. Mix all ingredients together using *pulse* only.

6 Give the mixture one final light stir with a spoon.

7 Drop mixture a teaspoon at a time onto a well-greased baking tray and bake for 8 to 10 minutes.

Hazel Delights
Makes 3 dozen

Imperial (Metric)	American
4 oz (115g) hazelnuts	¾ cup hazelnuts
6 fl oz (170ml) corn *or* sunflower oil	¾ cup corn *or* sunflower oil
4 oz (115g) clear honey	½ cup clear honey
½ teaspoon vanilla essence	½ teaspoon vanilla essence
Grated rind of 1 orange	Grated rind of 1 orange
8 oz (225g) wholemeal pastry flour	2 cups wholewheat pastry flour
Pinch sea salt (optional)	Pinch sea salt (optional)

1 Toast the hazelnuts in the oven at 350°F/180°C (Gas Mark 4), until lightly browned in the centre. Turn oven up to 400°F/200°C (Gas Mark 6).

2 Set *steel blades* in position and process nuts until finely ground. Take out.

3 Reset steel blades and blend oil and honey. Switch off motor.

4 Add vanilla essence, orange rind and ground hazelnuts and blend in, using *pulse*.

5 Add flour and sea salt and still using pulse blend well together.

6 Drop teaspoonsful of the mixture onto a well-greased baking tray, 2½ inches (6.5cm) apart and bake for 12 minutes. (Check after 9 minutes to ensure they do not burn.) Cool on the baking sheet.

Malted Sesame Biscuits
Makes 24

Imperial (Metric)	American
I heaped teaspoon bicarbonate of soda	I heaped teaspoon baking soda
2 teaspoons hot water	2 teaspoons hot water
5 oz (140g) polyunsaturated margarine	⅔ cup polyunsaturated margarine
I generous tablespoon malt extract	I generous tablespoon malt extract
3 oz (85g) fruit sugar	½ cup fruit sugar
A few drops natural vanilla essence	A few drops natural vanilla essence
3 oz (85g) sesame seeds	¾ cup sesame seeds
4 oz (115g) wholemeal pastry flour	I cup wholewheat pastry flour
3 oz (85g) porridge oats	¾ cup rolled oats

1 Heat oven to 300°F/150°C (Gas Mark 2).

2 Dissolve soda in the hot water.

3 Melt margarine and malt in a small saucepan over a pan of boiling water. Stir in sugar and keep warm until sugar has dissolved.

4 Add a few drops of vanilla essence to the warm liquid.

5 Set *steel blades* in position and put sesame seeds, flour and oats in the processor bowl. Process dry ingredients for a few seconds. Switch off motor.

6 Put soda mixture in the malt liquid and pour down the feed tube. Use *pulse* to mix all ingredients together. Do not over-mix.

7 Roll into small balls and put on a well-oiled baking tray 2 inches (5cm) apart to allow for spreading.

8 Bake for 20 to 25 minutes. Leave to get cold on the baking tray.

Seed and Honey Snaps
Makes 24

Imperial (Metric)	American
1 teaspoon bicarbonate of soda	1 teaspoon baking soda
2 teaspoons hot water	2 teaspoons hot water
2 tablespoons (30ml) clear honey	2 tablespoons clear honey
5 fl oz (140ml) sunflower oil	½ cup sunflower oil
2 oz (55g) fruit sugar	⅓ cup fruit sugar
1½ oz (45g) sunflower seeds	⅓ cup sunflower seeds
1½ oz (45g) pumpkin seeds	⅓ cup pumpkin seeds
3 oz (85g) medium oatmeal	¾ cup medium oatmeal
4 oz (115g) wholemeal flour	1 cup wholewheat flour
Pinch sea salt (optional)	Pinch sea salt (optional)
2 level teaspoons (10ml) ground ginger	2 level teaspoons ground ginger

1 Preheat oven to 300°F/150°C (Gas Mark 2).

2 Dissolve the soda in the hot water.

3 Heat honey, oil and sugar in a small saucepan over a pan of boiling water until sugar is dissolved.

4 Set *steel blades* in position and grind the seeds until they are like small breadcrumbs (*not* powdered).

5 Add oatmeal, flour, sea salt and ginger and mix together for a few seconds. Switch off motor.

6 Pour honey and oil mixture, plus soda mixture, down the feed tube and using *pulse* blend all ingredients together.

7 Roll into small balls and put on a well-oiled baking tray, 2 inches (5cm) apart to allow for spreading.

8 Bake 20 to 25 minutes. Let cool on the baking tray until crisp.

Variation:
Cashew and Cinnamon Snaps: Follow recipe and instructions as above, but omit the seeds and ginger and add cashew nuts and ground cinnamon.

Oatmeal Fruit and Nut Fingers

To fill a 10 inch (25cm) square shallow cake tin, well greased.

For the filling:

Imperial (Metric)	American
2 oz (55g) nuts (hazels or almonds)	½ cup of nuts (hazels or almonds)
2 oz (55g) sunflower seeds	⅓ cup sunflower seeds
4 oz (115g) dried apricots	⅔ cup dried apricots
4 oz (115g) dried figs	⅔ cup dried figs
4 oz (115g) stoned dates	⅔ cup pitted dates
½ teaspoon ground aniseed	½ teaspoon ground aniseed
½ teaspoon ground cinnamon	½ teaspoon ground cinnamon
¼ pint (140ml) apple juice	⅔ cup apple juice
2 tablespoons lemon juice	2 tablespoons lemon juice

For the oat mixture:

Imperial (Metric)	American
6 oz (170g) wholemeal flour	1½ cups wholewheat flour
8 oz (225g) porridge oats	2 cups rolled oats
12 oz (340g) polyunsaturated margarine	1½ cups polyunsaturated margarine

1 Set *steel blades* in position and grind nuts and seeds to a rough breadcrumb consistency. Take out and put in a mixing bowl.

2 Put apricots, figs, dates, spices and apple juice in a saucepan and cook on gentle heat until soft, about 15 minutes.

3 With steel blades still in position process fruit and lemon juice until pulp-like. Allow to cool. Clean and dry processor bowl.

4 Set steel blades back in position. Put flour, oats and margarine in the bowl and process for 30 seconds.

5 Press half this mixture into the bottom of the baking tin. Spread the fruit purée over this, then top with the remaining oat mixture.

6 Bake at 350°F/180°C (Gas Mark 4) for 20 to 25 minutes.

7 Cool in the tin and cut into fingers while still warm. Remove from the tin when quite cold.

6.

BABY TIME
The Right Start

As I mentioned in the introduction, whether we are on a meatless diet or not it is most important to know how to balance the food we eat, especially when catering for the very young if we wish them to grow into healthy adults. Not only have we to be aware of this balance but also of individual needs. Having had four children I must say that feeding our young can sometimes be a most frustrating experience. All those bibs and high chairs splattered with what we think is so good and necessary for them to eat. All that preparation and they won't eat it! My ignorance was certainly not bliss. Now I understand that they are individuals and their requirements in the very early stages, when solids are first introduced around the age of four to five months, are largely determined by their genetic make-up. These needs fluctuate from day to day and, as the child grows, the influence of their regular diet becomes paramount.

We all know that the way to encourage the general tendency towards sweet foods is to supply more sweet foods. The same is true with salt. Too much and you no longer taste the food but *need* to taste the salt. What we have to do is to try to educate the young palate to appreciate good food and not destroy the taste buds or overload their systems with de-vitalized, processed foods full of saturated fats, sugar and salt. We must give them instead food that will encourage the healthy growth of their bodies.

From the experience of my youngest child, I also realize that even when given a very wholesome diet she would sometimes prefer a piece of chocolate to dinner. Of course she doesn't often get that choice, but you cannot and should not block the world out. Let others treat them — and you, sometimes — but give them that super advantage of having good wholesome food most of the time and they too, like us, can enjoy a few indulgences. If nutritionally sound natural food is regular fare, then these foods will be what your baby will want to eat and enjoy when hungry.

It is only possible in the context of this book for me to give you a very brief guide to feeding your baby its first solids but there are a few very good books on the subject which are most enlightening and will help you greatly to understand the subject more fully.

From birth to one year

This chapter is not filled with recipes but will give you ideas for development that will make good use of your processor. It is important to read the notes and not just to try out random recipes.

The best start a child can have is a well-nourished and happy mother-to-be, not to mention a happy, well-nourished father, well-informed about pregnancy and birth. Everything you eat or drink will affect the growing foetus so it makes sense to feed yourself well and exercise if you are overweight, not cut down on nourishing foods. One of the most common ailments in pregnancy is anaemia, which is usually due to a deficiency in iron or folic acid. Eating foods rich in iron, such as beans, whole grains, the darker green vegetables, seaweed and kelp can help correct any iron deficiency.

The second best start is to feed your baby with breast milk for five months at least. The protein and fat in a mother's milk is more easily digested by the baby than the protein and fat in other substitutes.

Goat's milk is a reasonable alternative to mother's milk as it is easily digested by the infant. It does not have to be pasteurized, which destroys valuable nutrients and enzymes, because goats do not have the diseases of factory-reared cows and are not injected with antibiotics and hormones. Research has found that allergic conditions, asthma and eczema, have often been alleviated by the elimination of cow's milk and the addition of goat's milk to the diet.

Soya milk and all soya products are not advised until after seven months because the baby's digestive system is not ready for these foods until then. Tofu soya cheese (see page 38 on how to make), although easily digested, is very high in protein and needs diluting with plenty of liquid when first introduced.

Another food to be avoided before the baby is six months old is wheat, including wholemeal bread and any wheat-based cereal, because a child under this age is more likely to develop a gluten allergy.

It is also advisable to wait until the child is over seven months before including whole cow's milk, skimmed milk or egg whites as these foods have been found in some cases to cause allergic reactions.

Introducing foods to your baby

This is only from my experience, so remember the individuality of your child.

At around four months, start giving one teaspoonful of ripe mashed banana daily for one week. Then alternate this with one teaspoonful ripe mashed avocado pear the following week. The third week add two teaspoons of natural goat's milk yogurt to either the banana or avocado and give the banana and yogurt in the morning and the avocado early evening. Gradually increase the amount of these foods until the baby is about five months at which time an easily digested cereal such as millet, brown rice or oats can be introduced into the diet.

Cooking small amounts for one baby meal is a fiddle, so I suggest that you prepare larger amounts and freeze in ice-cube containers. A 1 inch (2.5cm) cube will be sufficient to add to fruit and yogurt to begin with.

First Two-Grain Cereal

Imperial (Metric)	American
4 oz (115g) Italian short grain brown rice, organically grown	½ cup Italian short grain brown rice, organically grown
3 oz (85g) raisins	½ cup raisins
4 oz (115g) whole grain millet	½ cup whole grain millet

1 Wash rice in a sieve by letting cold water run through the grains for one minute. Put rice in a heavy-based saucepan and add twice its volume in cold water plus half the raisins. Bring to boil, turn down to simmer and cook with a tight lid on for 35 to 40 minutes until quite soft.

2 In a dry, heavy-based saucepan toast millet, stirring constantly, until it smells nutty and is slightly browned.

3 Pour on 3 times its volume in boiling water, plus the remaining raisins, and simmer with a lid on for 20 minutes, or until all the grains are soft.

4 Set *steel blades* in position and process the rice and millet until the mixture is a smooth purée, adding a little more boiling water if necessary. Keep covered while cooling. When cold, spoon into ice-cube containers, slide into polythene bags and freeze. Defrost by putting the cubes in a small saucepan over a pan of boiling water.

Variations:
From this stage on, gradually add other vegetables and fruit such as steamed, mashed carrot or dried, soaked and puréed apricots, a spoonful at a time either mixed with a little of the cereal and/or yogurt, depending on how hungry your child is.

Nut, Seed and Apricot Cream

This recipe is a delicious nut, seed and fruit cream sauce the consistency of thick soup, which can be frozen in ice-cube containers and added to cereal or eaten as a sweet dish by itself. Apricots are a good source of iron; sesame seeds and almonds are rich in calcium.

Imperial (Metric)	American
2 oz (55g) dried, unsulphured apricots	⅓ cup dried, unsulphured apricots
Apple juice to soak apricots	Apple juice to soak apricots
2 oz (55g) whole almonds	½ cup whole almonds
2 oz (55g) sesame seeds	½ cup sesame seeds
1 pint (570ml) pure water	2½ cups pure water

1 Wash apricots well in boiling water and soak in a little apple juice overnight (keep covered).

2 Blanch almonds by pouring boiling water over them and peeling off skins when cool. Discard the water.

3 Set *steel blades* in position. Put sesame seeds and almonds into the processor bowl. Grind for 30 seconds and gradually pour in the pure water. Continue to process for two minutes more. Pour out of bowl and set *steel blades* back in position.

4 Put apricots and apple juice into the processor bowl and process until a smooth purée.

5 Pour nut and seed liquid through feed tube, while motor is running.

6 Blend well together. You should have a thick, soupy consistency. Spoon this into ice-cube containers and slide into polythene bags and freeze. Serve with cereal or by itself.

Variation:
Dates can be substituted for apricots. Just steam dates and blend in the processor with enough pure water to give a smooth consistency, and then add nut and seed liquid.

Six months and over

At over six months you can add vegetables like broccoli, cabbage and carrot. Steam all vegetables. Egg yolk can also be introduced, a teaspoonful only at first, puréed in the processor with a little steamed jacket potato and broccoli, cabbage or carrot. This makes a nourishing and substantial meal.

Tofu, the boon food for the vegetarian mother (see page 38 on making tofu) can be introduced at around seven months. It's great to stir into vegetable broths, mashed in potatoes or fruit purées. Again, give only one teaspoon to begin with, gradually increasing to 1 ounce (30g) at eight to nine months. Food at this stage and up until eight months must still be puréed but with a gradually higher concentration of ingredients and a thicker consistency.

Now I will give you a few recipes that can be safely eaten from eight months on.

Muesli

This simple recipe can be stored in an airtight container and eaten with fresh or dried puréed fruit and natural yogurt, goat's milk or cow's milk. Buy Muesli base, which comprises a variety of rolled grains, usually rye, millet, wheat, barley and oats.

Imperial (Metric)	American
3 oz (85g) sunflower seeds	½ cup sunflower seeds
2 oz (55g) raisins or sultanas	⅓ cup dark or golden seedless raisins
2 oz (55g) dried dates, figs or apricots	Just under ½ cup dried dates, figs or
10 oz (275g) Muesli base	apricots
	2½ cups Muesli base

1 Set *steel blades* in position. Put sunflower seeds in the processor bowl and process until powdery.

2 Roughly chop dried fruit.

3 Add muesli base and dried fruit to ground sunflower seeds and chop until the mixture is like very fine breadcrumbs. Keep in a screw-top jar.

Note: 2 tablespoons with yogurt or milk is ample at nine to ten months. Use less for babies under that age. A little finely grated eating apple is delicious with this cereal.

Nutritious Porridge

You can use various grains to make this porridge. I sometimes make it with Muesli base but porridge oats (not instant porridge) are usually in most store cupboards, so the recipe is based on these.

With *steel blades* grind the cereal to a powdery consistency for babies from six to nine months, then grind to a slightly rougher texture around the nine-month stage. Keep in a screw-top jar. Also grind enough sunflower and sesame seeds to last one week in a screw-top jar (no longer than this or they will become rancid-tasting). The recipe is an average portion at nine months.

Imperial (Metric)	American
I rounded tablespoon porridge oats, ground	I rounded tablespoon porridge oats, ground
I rounded teaspoon sesame and sunflower seeds, finely ground	I rounded teaspoon sesame and sunflower seeds, finely ground
5 tablespoons goat's milk or soya milk	5 tablespoons goat's milk or soy milk
½ level teaspoon Brewer's yeast	½ level teaspoon Brewer's yeast
½ teaspoon blackstrap molasses	½ teaspoon blackstrap molasses

1 Simply mix all ingredients together and cook on moderate heat in a small, heavy-based saucepan for 3 minutes only.

2 Serve with the following recipe for apple and apricot sauce.

Apple and Apricot Sauce

This sauce is delicious served with nut roast or with rice puddings, or the porridge above. Stored in screw-top jars in the fridge, it will last two to three weeks. For adults 1 crush two cardamon seeds to a fine powder and stir this into a small dishful when serving with a main meal. Choose thin skinned apples such as Golden Delicious or Cox's.

Imperial (Metric)	American
4 oz (115g) dried apricot pieces (unsulphured)	Just under 1 cup dried apricot pieces (unsulphured)
½ pint (285ml) apple juice	1⅓ cups apple juice
3 sweet dessert apples	3 sweet dessert apples

1 Wash apricots well in boiling water and soak in the apple juice overnight.

2 Core apples and chop. Leave skins on.

3 Place apricots, soaking juice and apples in a heavy-based saucepan and cook on moderate heat for 5 minutes only.

4 Set *steel blades* in position and process until the mixture is smooth.

5 Put into sterilized screw-top jars and store in the refrigerator. This sauce is delicious stirred into natural yogurt. A variation is to use prunes instead of apricots.

Soup

Soup is another easy food into which you can pack lots of goodness for children. You can freeze it in small containers, suitable for individual portions. To make a complete meal out of soup, cook grains, such as brown rice, buckwheat or millet. Add either 1 ounce (55g) tofu (see page 38 for recipe), 1 heaped tablespoon cottage cheese or 2 teaspoons of cooked beans such as aduki, mung or soya. For the final nutritional touch, stir in 1 heaped teaspoon wheatgerm.

I use *Vecon* in this soup recipe, which is a pure, savoury and delicious vegetable extract and its full-bodied flavour makes the soup enjoyable for our adult palates as well as children's. The mixture can also be used as a stock for dishes that require a gravy or sauce, or for stews.

Babies' Vegetable Broth (or Vegetable Stock)

Imperial (Metric)	American
3 inch (7.5cm) piece of kombu (sea vegetable)	3 inch piece of Kombu (sea vegetable)
1½ pints (850ml) water	3¾ cups water
1 medium onion, or leek when in season, roughly chopped	1 medium onion, or leek when in season, roughly chopped
2 medium carrots, roughly chopped	2 medium carrots, roughly chopped
2 sticks celery, roughly chopped	2 stalks celery, roughly chopped
2 medium potatoes, roughly chopped (leave skins on)	2 medium potatoes, roughly chopped (leave skins on)
3 oz (85g) green beans, roughly chopped	3 ounces green beans, roughly chopped
1 bunch watercress, roughly chopped	1 bunch watercress, roughly chopped
Large handful parsley, chopped	Large handful parsley, chopped
1 rounded teaspoon Vecon	1 rounded teaspoon Vecon

1 The kombu in dry form is in a stick shape which flattens out when soaked. Steep the kombu in the water for about 15 minutes.

2 Set *steel blades* in position and finely chop onion, carrots, celery, potatoes and green beans for 10 seconds only. This cuts down cooking time considerably.

3 Heat kombu and water to boiling point. Add other vegetables and simmer with the lid on for 15 minutes.

4 Chop watercress and parsley and add to soup mixture. Cook for 1 minute more only.

5 With *steel blades* in position process soup until very smooth. When quite cold put in small containers which hold approximately ¼ pint (140ml/⅔ cup).

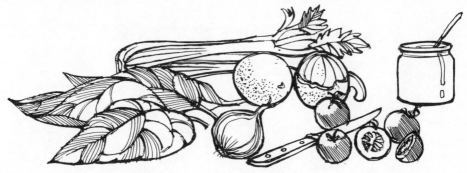

Take it from here

As you can see from the few recipes in this chapter, the variations are numerous. Children do not need gourmet meals — just simple, nutritious, naturally-seasoned foods which, of course, taste good to an unspoilt palate.

Leaving out highly spiced dishes, most of the recipes in the rest of the book are suitable in puréed or semi-puréed form after the age of ten months. So, if you eat well yourself it will naturally follow that, after the initial few months of specially-prepared foods, your baby will thrive on the food you give to the rest of the family. It is not only the child who needs a wholesome start — we all deserve the benefits to be gained from eating a healthy diet. The more thought we give to the food we eat, the more enjoyable the preparation and the eating becomes.

INDEX

By the same author

Evelyn Findlater's
NATURAL FOODS PRIMER

Here is a fascinating and appetizing introduction to the world of natural foods, including all the advice and information any cook needs to stock the kitchen with a whole harvest of goodness, and plan, prepare and cook delicious dishes for all types of meal and occasion using a wide variety of natural foods.

The carefully planned range of recipes are all clearly presented, and each new ingredient is simply explained, along with the reasons for choosing it in preference to processed food. All the recipes have been tried and tested by the author, by students at her adult cookery classes, and by children aged ten to fifteen — always with great success and enjoyment.

This is a book for every newcomer to natural foods, and a book to be used and enjoyed by all the family. With Evelyn Findlater's expert help, the discovery and use of natural foods will be both healthy and fun.